For:

_____

*Commit to the LORD whatever you do,
and your plans will succeed.*

PROVERBS 16:3

From:

_____

More of God's Words of Life for Men

Copyright 2002 by Zondervan

ISBN 0-310-80121-4

Requests for information should be addressed to:
Inspirio, The gift group of Zondervan
Grand Rapids, Michigan 49530
http://www.inspiriogifts.com

Compiler: Doris Rikkers
Project Manager: Janice Jacobson
Design Manager: Amy J. Wenger
Design: Kris Nelson

Printed in China
02 03 04/HK/ 4 3 2 1

MORE OF

God's Words
of Life
for
Men

from the
New International Version

Ψ

inspirio™

God's Words of Life On

Contents

God's Words of Life on
Acceptance

"Before I formed you in the womb I knew you, before you were born I set you apart," says the Lord.

JEREMIAH 1:5

Jesus said, "Come to me, all you who are weary and burdened, and I will give you rest. Take my yoke upon you and learn from me, for I am gentle and humble in heart, and you will find rest for your souls. For my yoke is easy and my burden is light."

MATTHEW 11:28–30

Whether we live or die, we belong to the Lord.

ROMANS 14:8

Because of his great love for us, God, who is rich in mercy, made us alive with Christ even when we were dead in transgressions—it is by grace you have been saved.

EPHESIANS 2:4–5

God's Words of Life on

Acceptance

This is how God showed his love among us: He sent his one and only Son into the world that we might live through him.

1 JOHN 4:9

God does not show favoritism but accepts men from every nation who fear him and do what is right.

ACTS 10:34–35

Accept one another, then, just as Christ accepted you, in order to bring praise to God.

ROMANS 15:7

God's favor lasts a lifetime;
weeping may remain for a night,
  but rejoicing comes in the morning.
When I felt secure, I said,
  "I will never be shaken."
O LORD, when you favored me,
  you made my mountain stand firm.

PSALM 30:5–7

We love because God first loved us.

1 JOHN 4:19

You created my inmost being;
  you knit me together in my mother's womb.
I praise you because I am fearfully and wonderfully made, O LORD;
  your works are wonderful,
  I know that full well.

PSALM 139:13-14

Praise be to the God and Father of our Lord
Jesus Christ, who has blessed us in the
heavenly realms with every spiritual blessing in
Christ. For he chose us in him before the
creation of the world to be holy and blameless
in his sight.

EPHESIANS 1:3–4

The Spirit himself testifies with our spirit that
we are God's children. Now if we are children,
then we are heirs—heirs of God and co-heirs
with Christ.

ROMANS 8:16–17

In contrast to the frustrated man who would like to run away from his responsibilities stands the redeemed man who feels safe and secure. He can be a shelter to others because he himself is sheltered. He is a man who has accepted himself not only with his strengths but also with his weaknesses. His secret: he knows he has been accepted by the Heavenly Father.

The redeemed man is a whole man. He is whole first because he belongs to a family, the family of God. God, his Father, makes him one of his sons.

He is a whole man because he feels worthy. Christ died to give him birth and therefore he can take as his own the worthiness of Christ.

He is a whole man because he feels competent. This competence comes from the Holy Spirit. "God did not give us a spirit of timidity, but a spirit of power, of love and of self-discipline" *(2 TIMOTHY 1:7)*.

WALTER TROBISCH

Ambition

Whatever was to my profit I now consider loss for the sake of Christ. What is more, I consider everything a loss compared to the surpassing greatness of knowing Christ Jesus my Lord, for whose sake I have lost all things. I consider them rubbish, that I may gain Christ.

PHILIPPIANS 3:7–8

It has always been my ambition to preach the gospel where Christ was not known, so that I would not be building on someone else's foundation.

ROMANS 15:20

Do you see a man skilled in his work?
  He will serve before kings;
  he will not serve before obscure men.

PROVERBS 22:29

Live a life worthy of the calling you have received.

EPHESIANS 4:1

Godliness with contentment is great gain.

1 TIMOTHY 6:6

Ambition

Make every effort to add to your faith goodness; and to goodness, knowledge; and to knowledge, self-control; and to self-control, perseverance; and to perseverance, godliness; and to godliness, brotherly kindness; and to brotherly kindness, love. For if you possess these qualities in increasing measure, they will keep you from being ineffective and unproductive in your knowledge of our Lord Jesus Christ. … Therefore, my brothers, be all the more eager to make your calling and election sure. For if you do these things, you will never fall, and you will receive a rich welcome into the eternal kingdom of our Lord and Savior Jesus Christ.

2 PETER 1:5–8, 10–11

God is not unjust; he will not forget your work and the love you have shown him as you have helped his people and continue to help them. We want each of you to show this same diligence to the very end, in order to make your hope sure.

HEBREWS 6:10–11

Do not store up for yourselves treasures on earth, where moth and rust destroy, and where thieves break in and steal. But store up for yourselves treasures in heaven, where moth and rust do not destroy, and where thieves do not break in and steal. For where your treasure is, there your heart will be also.

MATTHEW 6:19–21

God's Words of Life on
Ambition

There will be a resurrection of both the righteous and the wicked. So I strive always to keep my conscience clear before God and man.

ACTS 24:15–16

In everything that Hezekiah undertook in the service of God's temple and in obedience to the law and the commands, he sought his God and worked wholeheartedly. And so he prospered.

2 CHRONICLES 31:21

What good will it be for a man if he gains the whole world, yet forfeits his soul? Or what can a man give in exchange for his soul? For the Son of Man is going to come in his Father's glory with his angels, and then he will reward each person according to what he has done.

MATTHEW 16:26–27

Have faith in the LORD your God and you will be upheld.

2 CHRONICLES 20:20

Work done for personal gain dulls my spirit; work that produces something beyond myself excites me. Inviting God into my work opens the door for new creativity.

Being in the right job, doing the kind of work, where I give more than I receive, brings a whole new light onto my strength as a man.

LEONARD LESOURD

We must dispense with the myth that commitment to Christ means becoming a clergyman, or that work done inside a church building or in a church organization is more holy, some-how, than work done in the mar-ketplace. Christ came to give us a sense of calling in everyday work. This is where the world is changed, and where the kingdom is built.

BRUCE LARSON

God's Words of Life on
Attitude

Offer your bodies as living sacrifices, holy and pleasing to God—this is your spiritual act of worship. Do not conform any longer to the pattern of this world, but be transformed by the renewing of your mind. Then you will be able to test and approve what God's will is— his good, pleasing and perfect will.

ROMANS 12:1–2

Rejoice in the Lord always. I will say it again: Rejoice! Let your gentleness be evident to all. The Lord is near.

PHILIPPIANS 4:4–5

Man of God, . . . pursue righteousness, godliness, faith, love, endurance and gentleness. Fight the good fight of the faith. Take hold of the eternal life to which you were called when you made your good confession in the presence of many witnesses.

1 TIMOTHY 6:11–12

I heard the voice of the Lord saying, "Whom shall I send? And who will go for us?" And I said, "Here am I. Send me!"

ISAIAH 6:8

Attitude

Whatever is true, whatever is noble, whatever is right, whatever is pure, whatever is lovely, whatever is admirable—if anything is excellent or praiseworthy—think about such things.

PHILIPPIANS 4:8

Be on your guard; stand firm in the faith; be men of courage; be strong. Do everything in love.

1 CORINTHIANS 16:13–14

Jesus said, "Whoever wants to become great among you must be your servant, and whoever wants to be first must be slave of all. For even the Son of Man did not come to be served, but to serve, and to give his life as a ransom for many."

MARK 10:43–45

I watch in hope for the LORD,
  I wait for God my Savior; my God will hear me.

MICAH 7:7

You were taught, with regard to your former way of life, to put off your old self, which is being corrupted by its deceitful desires; to be made new in the attitude of your minds; and to put on the new self, created to be like God in true righteousness and holiness.

EPHESIANS 4:22–24

Since Christ suffered in his body, arm yourselves also with the same attitude, because he who has suffered in his body is done with sin. As a result, he does not live the rest of his earthly life for evil human desires, but rather for the will of God.

1 PETER 4:1–2

Your attitude should be the same as that of Christ Jesus: Who, being in very nature God, did not consider equality with God something to be grasped, but made himself nothing, taking the very nature of a servant, being made in human likeness. And being found in appearance as a man, he humbled himself and became obedient to death—even death on a cross!

PHILIPPIANS 2:5–8

All of you, clothe yourselves with humility toward one another, because, "God opposes the proud but gives grace to the humble." Humble yourselves, therefore, under God's mighty hand, that he may lift you up in due time.

1 PETER 5:5–6

I'm part of the fellowship of the unashamed. I have the Holy Spirit power. The die has been cast. I have stepped over the line. The decision has been made—I'm a disciple of his. I won't look back, let up, slow down, back away, or be still. My past is redeemed, my present makes sense, my future is secure. I'm finished and done with low living, sight walking, smooth knees, colorless dreams, tamed visions, worldly talking, cheap giving and dwarfed goals.

I no longer need preeminence, prosperity, position, promotions, plaudits or popularity. I don't have to be right, first, tops, recognized, praised, regarded or rewarded. I now live by faith, lean in his presence, walk by patience, am uplifted by prayer, and I labor with power.

A YOUNG PASTOR IN ZIMBABWE, AFRICA, LATER MARTYRED FOR HIS FAITH IN CHRIST.

Set your minds on things above, not on earthly things. For you died, and your life is now hidden with Christ in God. When Christ, who is your life, appears, then you also will appear with him in glory.

COLOSSIANS 3:2–4

Devotional Thought on
Attitude

The LORD bless you
and keep you;
the LORD make his face shine upon you
and be gracious to you;
the LORD turn his face toward you
and give you peace.

NUMBERS 6:24–26

O LORD, save us;
O LORD, grant us success.
Blessed is he who comes in the name of the
LORD.
From the house of the Lord we bless you.
The LORD is God,
and he has made his light shine upon us.

PSALM 118:25–27

Surely, O LORD, you bless the righteous;
you surround them with your favor as
with a shield.

PSALM 5:12

The blessing of the LORD brings wealth,
and he adds no trouble to it.

PROVERBS 10:22

Blessing

Jesus said, "Blessed are you when people insult you, persecute you and falsely say all kinds of evil against you because of me. Rejoice and be glad, because great is your reward in heaven, for in the same way they persecuted the prophets who were before you."

MATTHEW 5:11–12

Praise be to the God and Father of our Lord Jesus Christ, who has blessed us in the heavenly realms with every spiritual blessing in Christ.

EPHESIANS 1:3

Blessed is the man who perseveres under trial, because when he has stood the test, he will receive the crown of life that God has promised to those who love him.

JAMES 1:12

"I will bless them and the places surrounding my hill. I will send down showers in season; there will be showers of blessing," says the LORD.

EZEKIEL 34:26

Blessing

Blessed are the poor in spirit,
  for theirs is the kingdom of heaven.
Blessed are those who mourn,
  for they will be comforted.
Blessed are the meek,
  for they will inherit the earth.
Blessed are those who hunger and thirst for
    righteousness,
  for they will be filled.
Blessed are the merciful,
  for they will be shown mercy.
Blessed are the pure in heart,
  for they will see God.
Blessed are the peacemakers,
  for they will be called sons of God.
Blessed are those who are persecuted
    because of righteousness,
  for theirs is the kingdom of heaven.

MATTHEW 5:3–10

Blessed is he
  whose transgressions are forgiven,
  whose sins are covered.
Blessed is the man
  whose sin the LORD does not count against
  him and in whose spirit is no deceit.

PSALM 32:1–2

God's Words of Life on
Blessing

The same Lord is Lord of all and richly blesses all who call on him, for "Everyone who calls on the name of the Lord will be saved."

ROMANS 10:12–13

The LORD gives strength to his people;
  the LORD blesses his people with peace.

PSALM 29:11

All these blessings will come upon you and accompany you if you obey the LORD your God: You will be blessed in the city and blessed in the country. The fruit of your womb will be blessed, and the crops of your land and the young of your livestock—the calves of your herds and the lambs of your flocks. Your basket and your kneading trough will be blessed. You will be blessed when you come in and blessed when you go out. ... The LORD will send a blessing on your barns and on everything you put your hand to.

DEUTERONOMY 28:2–6, 8

From the fullness of God's grace we have all received one blessing after another.

JOHN 1:16

God's Words of Life on

Blessing

Blessed are all who fear the LORD,
  who walk in his ways.
You will eat the fruit of your labor;
  blessings and prosperity will be yours.

PSALM 128:1–2

Though I am free and belong to no man, I
make myself a slave to everyone, to win as
many as possible. ... I do all this for the sake
of the gospel, that I may share in
its blessings.

1 CORINTHIANS 9:19, 23

Grace and peace to you from God the Father
and the Lord Jesus Christ.

2 THESSALONIANS 1:2

O LORD Almighty,
  blessed is the man who trusts in you.

PSALM 84:12

Solomon, the writer of Psalm 127, compares the home to a city. When an ancient city was built, it was not uncommon for the walls to be finished first to keep out the enemy. If the people trusted in the walls to protect them, to give them security, their trust was misplaced, creating only a false sense of security. Likewise, walls we erect around our families and possessions offer only an illusion of security. Ultimately, it is not the watchman or the walls that protect the people; it is the Lord! In the same sense, unless a husband and wife trust in God, their work and their watchfulness are wasted. Many feel that by working longer hours they can provide more things to bring happiness to their home or afford a nicer, newer home in hopes that it will bring happiness. But these things don't satisfy that empty longing in the pit of our souls, that longing for a home, a real home—a home where love thrives, lush and fragrant. The reason why it's futile to burn the candle at both ends—rising early, staying up late—is that God, not our labors, is the source of our blessing, as Psalm 127:2 indicates: "for he grants sleep to those he loves" [or, as another translation reads, "for while they sleep he provides for those he loves"].

CHARLES SWINDOLL

Change

Jesus Christ is the same yesterday and today and forever.

HEBREWS 13:8

Whatever is has already been,
  and what will be has been before;
  and God will call the past to account.

ECCLESIASTES 3:15

I the LORD do not change.

MALACHI 3:6

My soul finds rest in God alone;
  my salvation comes from him.
He alone is my rock and my salvation;
  he is my fortress, I will never be shaken.

PSALM 62:1–2

Every good and perfect gift is from above,
coming down from the Father of the heavenly
lights, who does not change like
shifting shadows.

JAMES 1:17

God's Words of Life on
Change

The plans of the LORD stand firm forever,
  the purposes of his heart
  through all generations.

PSALM 33:11

If anyone is in Christ, he is a new creation;
the old has gone, the new
has come!

2 CORINTHIANS 5:17

Listen, I tell you a mystery: We will not all
sleep, but we will all be changed—in a flash,
in the twinkling of an eye, at the last trumpet.
For the trumpet will sound, the dead will be
raised imperishable, and we will be changed.

1 CORINTHIANS 15:51–52

I have set the LORD always before me.
  Because he is at my right hand,
  I will not be shaken.

PSALM 16:8

God's Words of Life on
Change

There is a time for everything,

and a season for every activity under heaven:

a time to be born and a time to die,

a time to plant and a time to uproot,

a time to kill and a time to heal,

a time to tear down and a time to build,

a time to weep and a time to laugh,

a time to mourn and a time to dance,

a time to scatter stones and a time to
  gather them,

a time to embrace and a time to refrain

a time to search and a time to give up,

a time to keep and a time to throw away,

a time to tear and a time to mend,

a time to be silent and a time to speak,

a time to love and a time to hate,

a time for war and a time for peace.

ECCLESIASTES 3:1—8

Exile (being where we don't want to be with people we don"t want to be with) forces a decision: Will I focus my attention on what is wrong with the world and feel sorry for myself? Or will I focus my energies on how I can live at my best in this place I find myself?

Change is hard. Developing intimacy among strangers is always a risk. Building relationships in unfamiliar and hostile surroundings is difficult. All of us are given moments, days, months, years of exile. What will we do with them? Wish we were someplace else? Complain? Escape into fantasies? Drug ourselves into oblivion? Or build and plant and marry and seek the shalom of the place we inhabit and the people we are with? Exile reveals what really matters and frees us to pursue what really matters, which is to seek the Lord with all our hearts.

EUGENE H. PETERSON

Devotional Thought on

Change

We also rejoice in our sufferings, because we know that suffering produces perseverance; perseverance, character; and character, hope.

ROMANS 5:3—4

Do your best to present yourself to God as one approved, a workman who does not need to be ashamed and who correctly handles the word of truth.

2 TIMOTHY 2:15

Who may ascend the hill of the LORD?
  Who may stand in his holy place?
He who has clean hands and a pure heart,
  who does not lift up his soul to an idol
  or swear by what is false.

PSALM 24:3—4

Good will come to him who is generous
    and lends freely,
    who conducts his affairs with justice.
Surely he will never be shaken;
    a righteous man will be remembered forever.

PSALM 112:5-6

God's Words of Life on
Character

Love the LORD your God with all your heart
and with all your soul and with all your
strength. These commandments that I give
you today are to be upon your hearts.
Impress them on your children. Talk about
them when you sit at home and when you
walk along the road, when you lie down and
when you get up.

DEUTERONOMY 6:5–7

He has showed you, O man, what is good.
  and what does the LORD require of you?
To act justly and to love mercy
  and to walk humbly with your God.

MICAH 6:8

Blessed is the man
  who does not walk in the counsel
  of the wicked
or stand in the way of sinners
  or sit in the seat of mockers.
But his delight is in the law of the LORD
  and on his law he meditates day and night.

PSALM 1:1–2

Who is wise and understanding among you?
Let him show it by his good life, by deeds
done in the humility that comes from wisdom.

JAMES 3:13

Be careful to do what the LORD your God has
commanded you; do not turn aside to the
right or to the left. Walk in all the way that
the LORD your God has commanded you, so
that you may live and prosper and prolong
your days.

DEUTERONOMY 5:32–33

Pursue righteousness, faith, love and peace,
along with those who call on the LORD of a
pure heart.

2 TIMOTHY 2:22

Do nothing out of selfish ambition or vain
conceit, but in humility consider others better
than yourselves.

PHILIPPIANS 2:3–4

Some of a person's character is developed as a child. It's the result of values learned from family and other significant people early in life—which is what makes our role as parents and the role of those who coach kids so important.

We also develop character by going through adversity. Coaches sometimes talk about a losing year being a "character-building season." There's truth to that as I've seen from experience. That strength of character so crucial to the 1970 Dallas Cowboys who rallied from almost certain failure to go on to the Super Bowl was forged through those difficult years when we couldn't win the big one.

They were perfect illustration of what the apostle Paul was saying: "We know that suffering produces perseverance; perseverance, character; and character, hope" (Romans 5:3–4).

TOM LANDRY

Devotional Thought on
Character

Comfort

"As a mother comforts her child,
   so will I comfort you," says the LORD.

ISAIAH 66:13

Praise be to the God and Father of our Lord
Jesus Christ, the Father of compassion and the
God of all comfort, who comforts us in all our
troubles, so that we can comfort those in any
trouble with the comfort we ourselves have
received from God.

2 CORINTHIANS 1:3-4

Cast your cares on the LORD
   and he will sustain you;
   he will never let the righteous fall.

PSALM 55:22

We know that in all things God works for the good
of those who love him, who have been called
according to his purpose.

ROMANS 8:28

God's Words of Life on
Comfort

Blessed are those who mourn,
 for they will be comforted.

MATTHEW 5:4

"Even to your old age and gray hairs
 I am he, I am he who will sustain you.
I have made you and I will carry you;
 I will sustain you and I will rescue you,"
 says the Lord.

ISAIAH 46:4

Jesus said, "Now is your time of grief, but I
will see you again and you will rejoice, and no
one will take away your joy."

JOHN 16:22

Give me a sign of your goodness,
 that my enemies may see it
 and be put to shame,
 for you, O Lord, have helped me
 and comforted me.

PSALM 86:17

Comfort

Jesus said, "Do not let your hearts be troubled. Trust in God; trust also in me."

JOHN 14:1

Let us . . . approach the throne of grace with confidence, so that we may receive mercy and find grace to help us in our time of need.

HEBREWS 4:16

I will praise you, O LORD.
  Although you were angry with me,
your anger has turned away
  and you have comforted me.

ISAIAH 12:1

Jesus said, "My grace is sufficient for you, for my power is made perfect in weakness."

2 CORINTHIANS 12:9

Weeping may remain for a night,
  but rejoicing comes in the morning.

PSALM 30:5

God's Words of Life on
Comfort

Who, O God, is like you?
Though you have made me see troubles,
 many and bitter,
 you will restore my life again;
 from the depths of the earth
 you will again bring me up.
You will increase my honor
 and comfort me once again.

PSALM 71:19–21

Jesus said, "I am the resurrection and the
life. He who believes in me will live, even
though he dies."

JOHN 11:25

My comfort in my suffering is this:
 Your promise preserves my life, O LORD.

PSALM 119:50

Jesus said, "In this world you will have
trouble. But take heart! I have
overcome the world."

JOHN 16:33

Jesus said, "Come to me, all you who are weary and burdened, and I will give you rest."

MATTHEW 11:28

We are hard pressed on every side, but not crushed; perplexed, but not in despair; persecuted, but not abandoned; struck down, but not destroyed. We always carry around in our body the death of Jesus, so that the life of Jesus may also be revealed in our body.

2 CORINTHIANS 4:8–10

The LORD is the everlasting God,
  the Creator of the ends of the earth.
He will not grow tired or weary,
  and his understanding no one can fathom.
He gives strength to the weary
  and increases the power of the weak.
Those who hope in the LORD
  will renew their strength.
They will soar on wings like eagles;
  they will run and not grow weary,
  they will walk and not be faint.

ISAIAH 40:28–29, 31

When life caves in, you do not need reasons, you need comfort. You do not need some answers; you need someone. And Jesus does not come to us with an explanation; he comes to us with his presence.

We are always seeking the reason. We want to know why. Like Job, we finally want God to tell us just what is going on.

But God does not reveal his plan, he reveals himself. He comes to us as warmth when we are cold, fellowship when we are alone, strength when we are weak, peace when we are troubled, courage when we are afraid, songs when we are sad, and bread when we are hungry.

He is with us on our journeys. He is there when we are home. He sits with us at our table. He knows about funerals and weddings and commencements and hospitals and jails and unemployment and labor and laughter and rest and tears. He knows because he is with us. He comes to us again and again.

BOB BENSON

Devotional Thought on

Comfort

May the words of my mouth and the
meditation of my heart
be pleasing in your sight,
O LORD, my Rock and my Redeemer.

PSALM 19:14

A man of knowledge uses words
with restraint,
and a man of understanding is
even-tempered.

PROVERBS 17:27

A word aptly spoken
is like apples of gold in settings of silver.

PROVERBS 25:11

The quiet words of the wise are more to be
heeded
than the shouts of a ruler of fools.

ECCLESIASTES 9:17

The heavens declare the glory of God;
  the skies proclaim the work of his hands.
Day after day they pour forth speech;
  night after night they display knowledge.
There is no speech or language
  where their voice is not heard.
Their voice goes out into all the earth.
  their words to the ends of the world.

PSALM 19:1–4

Pleasant words are a honeycomb,
  sweet to the soul and healing to the bones.

PROVERBS 16:24

Let your conversation be always full of grace,
seasoned with salt, so that you may know
how to answer everyone.

COLOSSIANS 4:6

Words from a wise man's mouth
  are gracious.

ECCLESIASTES 10:12

He who guards his lips guards his life.

PROVERBS 13:3

Speak to one another with psalms, hymns and spiritual songs. Sing and make music in your heart to the Lord.

EPHESIANS 5:19

I do not hide your righteousness in my heart;
I speak of your faithfulness and salvation.
I do not conceal your love and your truth
  from the great assembly.
Do not withhold your mercy from me,
  O LORD; may your love and your truth always
  protect me.

PSALM 40:10–11

God's Words of Life on
Communication

Fix these words of mine in your hearts and minds; tie them as symbols on your hands and bind them on your foreheads. Teach them to your children, talking about them when you sit at home and when you walk along the road, when you lie down and when you get up. Write them on the doorframes of your houses and on your gates, so that your days and the days of your children may be many in the land that the LORD swore to give your forefathers, as many as the days that the heavens are above the earth.

DEUTERONOMY 11:18–21

From the fruit of his lips a man is filled with
 good things
as surely as the work of his hands rewards
 him.

PROVERBS 12:14

Speaking the truth in love, we will in all things grow up into him who is the Head, that is, Christ.

EPHESIANS 4:15

God's Words of Life on
Communication

LORD , who may dwell in your sanctuary?
  Who may live on your holy hill?
He whose walk is blameless
  and who does what is righteous,
who speaks the truth from his heart.

PSALM 15:1–2

The mouth of the righteous man
    utters wisdom,
  and his tongue speaks what is just
The law of his God is in his heart;
  his feet do not slip.

PSALM 37:30–31

He who guards his mouth and his tongue
  keeps himself from calamity.

PROVERBS 21:23

He who loves a pure heart and whose speech
  is gracious
    will have the king for his friend.

PROVERBS 22:11

Fidelity means a stubborn dedication to growth in personal relationship. Personal relationships are nourished only through communication, and communication between two people can be very difficult to maintain. For one thing, it takes time. And, above all, it takes desire. Personal communication is difficult because it is painful for us to talk about what we are feeling. It is much easier to discuss the unbalanced checking account than to discuss how we feel toward each other. But more, it is difficult because when we talk we are not sure what becomes of our message after it is filtered through the receptive apparatus of the person who receives it. Fidelity will give us the job of finding out what the other person is actually hearing from us and of patiently probing what the other person is actually trying to say.

LEWIS SMEDES

Devotional Thought on
Communication

I have learned to be content whatever the circumstances. I know what it is to be in need, and I know what it is to have plenty. I have learned the secret of being content in any and every situation, whether well fed or hungry, whether living in plenty or in want. I can do everything through Christ who gives me strength.

PHILIPPIANS 4:11–13

Better a little with the fear of the LORD
  than great wealth with turmoil.

PROVERBS 15:16

Satisfy us in the morning with your unfailing
  love, O LORD,
that we may sing for joy and be glad
  all our days.

PSALM 90:14

Godliness with contentment is great gain.

1 TIMOTHY 6:6

The fear of the LORD leads to life:
  Then one rests content,
  untouched by trouble.

PROVERBS 19:23

Do not store up for yourselves treasures on earth, where moth and rust destroy, and where thieves break in and steal. But store up for yourselves treasures in heaven, where moth and rust do not destroy, and where thieves do not break in and steal. For where your treasure is, there your heart will be also.

MATTHEW 6:19–21

Praise the LORD, O my soul,
  and forget not all his benefits—
who forgives all your sins
  and heals all your diseases,
who redeems your life from the pit
  and crowns you with love and compassion,
who satisfies your desires with good things
  so that your youth is renewed like the
    eagle's.

PSALM 103:2–5

Keep your lives free from the love of money and be content with what you have, because God has said,
  "Never will I leave you;
  never will I forsake you."

HEBREWS 13:5

You still the hunger of those you cherish,
  LORD; their sons have plenty,
  and they store up wealth for their children.
And I—in righteousness I will see your face;
  when I awake, I will be satisfied with
    seeing your likeness.

PSALM 17:14–15

Because your love is better than life, O LORD,
  my lips will glorify you.
I will praise you as long as I live,
  and in your name I will lift up my hands.
My soul will be satisfied as with the
  richest of foods;
  with singing lips my mouth will praise you.

PSALM 63:3–5

Let [the redeemed] give thanks to the LORD
    for his unfailing love
  and his wonderful deeds for men,
for he satisfies the thirsty
  and fills the hungry with good things.

PSALM 107:8–9

The sooner a man becomes satisfied with what he has and stops comparing his financial scorecard and trophies with those of other men, the better he will feel about himself. The apostle Paul states: "I have learned to be content whatever the circumstances. I know what it is to be in need, and I know what it is to have plenty. I have learned the secret of being content in any and every situation, whether well fed or hungry, whether living in plenty or in want" (Philippians 4:11–12). Men who opt to be satisfied with what they possess will have more time and energy for the kinds of nurturing relationships that will meet their basic needs.

STEPHEN ARTERBURN AND DAVID STOOP

Give me neither poverty nor riches,
  But give me only my daily bread.

PROVERBS 30:8

Devotional Thought on
Contentment

Be strong and courageous. Do not be terrified; do not be discouraged, for the LORD your God will be with you wherever you go.

JOSHUA 1:9

Though an army besiege me,
  my heart will not fear;
though war break out against me,
  even then will I be confident.

PSALM 27:3

The LORD is with me; I will not be afraid.
  What can man do to me?

PSALM 118:6

God did not give us a spirit of timidity, but a spirit of power, of love and of self-discipline.

2 TIMOTHY 1:7

The LORD is my light and my salvation—
  whom shall I fear?
The LORD is the stronghold of my life—
  of whom shall I be afraid?

PSALM 27:1

Who shall separate us from the love of
Christ? Shall trouble or hardship or persecution or famine or nakedness or danger or
sword? ... No, in all these things we are
more than conquerors through him who loved
us. For I am convinced that neither death nor
life, neither angels nor demons, neither the
present nor the future, nor any powers,
neither height nor depth, nor anything else in
all creation, will be able to separate us from
the love of God that is in Christ Jesus our
Lord.

ROMANS 8:35, 37–39

Be strong and take heart,
 all you who hope in the LORD.

PSALM 31:24

When you lie down, you will not be afraid;
   when you lie down, your sleep will be sweet.
Have no fear of sudden disaster
   or of the ruin that overtakes the wicked,
   for the LORD will be your confidence
   and will keep your foot from being snared.

PROVERBS 3:24–26

I am still confident of this:
   I will see the goodness of the LORD
   in the land of the living.
Wait for the LORD;
   be strong and take heart
   and wait for the LORD.

PSALM 27:13–14

The Lord the strength of his people,
   a fortress of salvation for his anointed one.

PSALM 28:8

Give me courage Lord
to take risks
not the usual ones
respected
necessary
relatively safe
but those I could avoid
the go-for-broke ones.
I need courage
not just because
I may fall on my face
or worse
but others seeing me
a sorry spectacle
if it should happen
will say
he didn't know what he was doing
or he's foolhardy ...
When it comes right down to it, Lord
I choose to be your failure
before anyone else's success.
Keep me from reneging
on my choice.

JOSEPH BAYLY

Buy the truth and do not sell it;
  get wisdom, discipline and understanding.

PROVERBS 23:23

Blessed is the man whom God corrects;
so do not despise the discipline
  of the Almighty.

JOB 5:17

He who heeds discipline shows the way to life.

PROVERBS 10:17

O LORD, you are our Father.
  We are the clay, you are the potter;
  we are all the work of your hand.

ISAIAH 64:8

Let the word of Christ dwell in you richly as
you teach and admonish one another with all
wisdom, and as you sing psalms, hymns and
spiritual songs with gratitude in your hearts to
God.

COLOSSIANS 3:16

God's Words of Life on
Discipline

Blessed is the man you discipline, O LORD,
the man you teach from your law;
you grant him relief from days of trouble.

PSALM 94:12–13

"Do not make light of the Lord's discipline,
and do not lose heart when he rebukes you,
because the Lord disciplines those he loves,
and he punishes everyone he accepts as a
son." Endure hardship as discipline; God is
treating you as sons. For what son is not disciplined by his father? ... Moreover, we have
all had human fathers who disciplined us and
we respected them for it. How much more
should we submit to the Father of our spirits
and live! Our fathers disciplined us for a little
while as they thought best; but God disciplines
us for our good, that we may share in his holiness. No discipline seems pleasant at the
time, but painful. Later on, however, it produces a harvest of righteousness and peace
for those who have been trained by it.

HEBREWS 12:5–7, 9–11

God's Words of Life on
Discipline

These commands are a lamp,
  this teaching is a light,
and the corrections of discipline
  are the way to life.

PROVERBS 6:23

A fool spurns his father's discipline,
but whoever heeds correction
  shows prudence.

PROVERBS 15:5

Whoever loves discipline loves knowledge,
  but he who hates correction is stupid.

PROVERBS 12:1

Jesus said, "Those whom I love I rebuke and
discipline. So be earnest, and repent."

REVELATION 3:19

As a Christian, I run into the very same problems on a spiritual level that I do on the football field. I can get blindsided by friends or other people who don't understand me and what I stand for. I've been attacked for my beliefs by a double-team and a triple-team. How do I handle these threats to my faith? The same way I do as a football player.

The first step is to discipline myself through training. I must study God's Word on a daily basis. Paul wrote to Timothy; "Do your best to present yourself to God as one approved, a workman who does not need to be ashamed and who correctly handles the word of truth" (2 Timothy 2:15). There is no way I will ever be able to deal with all that life has to offer without daily and diligently delving into God's Word.

The second focus is on my surroundings. I must also be careful not to surround myself too closely with those who don't believe in God's Word. It doesn't take too much sense to realize that you become like those with whom you spend the most time. Know your surroundings and control them; don't let your surroundings control you.

Finally, practice what you know is right. Too often we focus on doing what we've always done. We don't progress, keep in shape, work out daily. The warning is clear: "Solid food is for the mature, who by constant use have trained themselves to distinguish good from evil. Therefore let us leave the elementary teachings about Christ and go on to maturity" (Hebrews 5:14—6:1).

REGGIE WHITE

Devotional Thought on **Discipline**

Consider it pure joy, my brothers, whenever you face trials of many kinds, because you know that the testing of your faith develops perseverance. Perseverance must finish its work so that you may be mature and complete, not lacking anything.

JAMES 1:2-4

I cry aloud to the LORD;
 I lift up my voice to the LORD for mercy,
I pour out my complaint before him;
 before him I tell my trouble.
When my spirit grows faint within me,
 it is you who know my way.

PSALM 142:1–3

Praise be to the God and Father of our Lord Jesus Christ! In his great mercy he has given us new birth into a living hope through the resurrection of Jesus Christ from the dead. … In this you greatly rejoice, though now for a little while you may have had to suffer grief in all kinds of trials.

1 PETER 1:3, 6

God's Words of Life on
Encouragement

The LORD is my light and my salvation—
  whom shall I fear?
The LORD is the stronghold of my life—
  of whom shall I be afraid? ...
Though an army besiege me,
  my heart will not fear;
though war break out against me,
  even then will I be confident.

PSALM 27:1, 3

Jesus said, "Do not let your hearts be troubled. Trust in God; trust also in me. In my Father's house are many rooms; if it were not so, I would have told you. I am going there to prepare a place for you. And if I go and prepare a place for you, I will come back and take you to be with me that you also may be where I am."

JOHN 14:1–3

Be strong and do not give up, for your work will be rewarded.

2 CHRONICLES 15:7

Strengthen the feeble hands,
  steady the knees that give way;
say to those with fearful hearts,
  "Be strong, do not fear;
your God will come,
  he will come with vengeance;
with divine retribution
  he will come to save you.

ISAIAH 35:3–4

We do not lose heart. Though outwardly we are wasting away, yet inwardly we are being renewed day by day. For our light and momentary troubles are achieving for us an eternal glory that far outweighs them all. So we fix our eyes not on what is seen, but on what is unseen. For what is seen is temporary, but what is unseen is eternal.

2 CORINTHIANS 4:16–18

You hear, O Lord, the desire of the afflicted;
  you encourage them, and you listen to their
  cry.

PSALM 10:17

God's Words of Life on
Encouragement

Let us hold unswervingly to the hope we profess, for God who promised is faithful. And let us consider how we may spur one another on toward love and good deeds. Let us not give up meeting together, as some are in the habit of doing, but let us encourage one another.

HEBREWS 10:23–25

You are a shield around me, O LORD;
  you bestow glory on me and lift up my head.
To the LORD I cry aloud,
  and he answers me from his holy hill.

PSALM 3:3–4

Bring joy to your servant,
  for to you, O LORD,
  I lift up my soul.
You are forgiving and good, O LORD,
  abounding in love to all who call to you.

PSALM 86:4–5

I lift up my eyes to the hills—
  where does my help come from?
My help comes from the LORD,
  the Maker of heaven and earth.
He will not let your foot slip—
  he who watches over you will not slumber;
indeed, he who watches over Israel
  will neither slumber nor sleep.
The LORD watches over you—
  the LORD is your shade at your right hand;
the sun will not harm you by day,
  nor the moon by night.
The LORD will keep you from all harm—
  he will watch over your life;
the LORD will watch over your coming and
  going both now and forevermore.

PSALM 121

At the moment of rebirth, when the human spirit is "yielded and still," the Holy Spirit moves in to make his home and to provide assistance for our pilgrimage with God.

He becomes our Guide: David prays, "Show me the way" (Psalm 143:8), sensing that God's guiding Spirit will not leave him stranded.

He becomes our Enabler: "Rescue me from my enemies" (Psalm 143:9), David continues. It is the Spirit of God who enables and empowers.

He becomes our Teacher: "Teach me to do your will ... may your good Spirit lead me on level ground" (Psalm 143:10). The Holy Spirit is our Teacher/Interpreter. It is he who explains spiritual mysteries and levels the ground for our understanding.

He becomes our Comforter: "For your name's sake, O Lord, preserve my life ... bring me out of trouble" (Psalm 143:11). God's Spirit whispers words of encouragement and calls to our minds his mighty works in our behalf. He banishes discouragement and puts a song in our hearts!

DON WYRTZEN

Devotional Thought on

Encouragement

God's Words of Life on
Faith

Everything is possible for him who believes.

MARK 9:23

Faith is being sure of what we hope for and certain of what we do not see. ... And without faith it is impossible to please God, because anyone who comes to him must believe that he exists and that he rewards those who earnestly seek him.

HEBREWS 11:1, 6

Jesus said, "Blessed are those who have not seen and yet have believed."

JOHN 20:29

If you confess with your mouth, "Jesus is Lord," and believe in your heart that God raised him from the dead, you will be saved.

ROMANS 10:9

Everyone born of God overcomes the world. This is the victory that has overcome the world, even our faith.

1 JOHN 5:4

God's Words of Life on
Faith

If you believe, you will receive whatever you ask for in prayer.

MATTHEW 21:22

Since we have been justified through faith, we have peace with God through our Lord Jesus Christ.

ROMANS 5:1

To all who received Jesus, to those who believed in his name, he gave the right to become children of God—children born not of natural descent, nor of human decision or a husband's will, but born of God.

JOHN 1:12-13

We live by faith, not by sight.

2 CORINTHIANS 5:7

Jesus said, "I tell you the truth, if you have faith as small as a mustard seed, you can say to this mountain, 'Move from here to there' and it will move. Nothing will be impossible for you."

MATTHEW 17:20

Faith

Just as you received Christ Jesus as Lord,
continue to live in him, rooted and built up in
him, strengthened in the faith as you were
taught, and overflowing with thankfulness.

COLOSSIANS 2:6–7

Take up the shield of faith, with which you can
extinguish all the flaming arrows of the
evil one.

EPHESIANS 6:16

It is by faith you stand firm.

2 CORINTHIANS 1:24

Let us fix our eyes on Jesus, the author and
perfecter of our faith who for the joy set
before him endured the cross, scorning its
shame, and sat down at the right hand of the
throne of God.

HEBREWS 12:2

Faith comes from hearing the message, and
the message is heard through the word of
Christ.

ROMANS 10:17

God's Words of Life on
Faith

Make very effort to add to your faith goodness; and to goodness, knowledge; and to
knowledge self-control; and to self-control,
perseverance; and to perseverance, godliness; and to godliness, brotherly kindness;
and to brotherly kindness, love. For if you
possess these qualities in increasing measure, they will keep you from being ineffective
and unproductive in your knowledge of our
Lord Jesus Christ.

2 PETER 1:5–8

In the gospel a righteousness from God is
revealed, a righteousness that is by faith from
first to last, just as it is written: "The
righteous will live by faith."

ROMANS 1:17

By faith Moses, when he had grown up,
refused to be known as the son of Pharaoh's
daughter. He chose to be mistreated along
with the people of God rather than to enjoy
the pleasures of sin for a short time. He
regarded disgrace for the sake of Christ as of
greater value than the treasures of Egypt,
because he was looking ahead to his reward.

HEBREWS 11:24–26

God's Words of Life on
Faith

All these people [Noah, Jacob, Abraham] were still living by faith when they died. They did not receive the things promised; they only saw them and welcomed them from a distance. And they admitted that they were aliens and strangers on earth. People who say such things show that they are looking for a country of their own. If they had been thinking of the country they had left, they would have had opportunity to return. Instead, they were longing for a better country—a heavenly one. Therefore God is not ashamed to be called their God, for he has prepared a city for them.

HEBREWS 11:13–16

Though you have not seen Jesus, you love him; and even though you do not see him now, you believe in him and are filled with an inexpressible and glorious joy, for you are receiving the goal of your faith, the salvation of your souls.

1 PETER 1:8–9

Obedience is the key to real faith—the unshakable kind of faith so powerfully illustrated by Job's life. Job lost his home, his family (except for a nagging wife), his health, even his hope.

This is real faith: believing and acting obediently regardless of circumstances or contrary evidence. After all, if faith depended on visible evidence, it wouldn't be faith.

It is absurd for Christians to constantly seek new demonstrations of God's power, to expect a miraculous answer to every need, from curing ingrown toenails to finding parking spaces; this only leads to faith in miracles rather than the Maker.

True faith depends not upon mysterious signs, celestial fireworks, or grandiose dispensations from a God who is seen as a rich, benevolent uncle; true faith, as Job understood, rests on the assurance that God is who he is. Indeed, on that we must be willing to stake our very lives.

CHARLES COLSON

Devotional Thought on

Faith

Who is a God like you,
  who pardons sin and forgives the transgression
  of the remnant of his inheritance?
You do not stay angry forever
  but delight to show mercy.

MICAH 7:18

Praise the LORD, O my soul,
  and forget not all his benefits—
  who forgives all your sins
  and heals all your diseases.

PSALM 103:2-3

In Christ we have redemption through his
blood, the forgiveness of sins, in accordance
with the riches of God's grace.

EPHESIANS 1:7

If we confess our sins, God is faithful and just
and will forgive us our sins and purify us from
all unrighteousness.

1 JOHN 1:9

Seek the LORD while he may be found;
  call on him while he is near.
Let the wicked forsake his way
  and the evil man his thoughts.
Let him turn to the LORD, and he will have
    mercy on him,
  and to our God, for he will freely pardon.

ISAIAH 55:6–7

If you forgive men when they sin against you,
your heavenly Father will also forgive you.

MATTHEW 6:14

Be kind and compassionate to one another,
forgiving each other, just as in Christ God
forgave you.

EPHESIANS 4:32

You are a forgiving God, gracious and
compassionate, slow to anger and abounding
in love.

NEHEMIAH 9:17

O you who hear prayer,
  to you all men will come, LORD.
When we were overwhelmed by sins,
  you forgave our transgressions.

PSALM 65:2–3

Bear with each other and forgive whatever
grievances you may have against one another.
Forgive as the Lord forgave you.

COLOSSIANS 3:13

If you, O LORD, kept a record of sins,
  O Lord, who could stand?
But with you there is forgiveness;
  therefore you are feared.

PSALM 130:3–4

"If my people, who are called by my name, will
humble themselves and pray and seek my
face and turn from their wicked ways, then
will I hear from heaven and will forgive their
sin and will heal their land," says the Lord.

2 CHRONICLES 7:14

When you were dead in your sins and in the uncircumcision of your sinful nature, God made you alive with Christ. He forgave us all our sins, having canceled the written code, with its regulations, that was against us and that stood opposed to us; he took it away, nailing it to the cross.

COLOSSIANS 2:13–14

[The Father] has qualified you to share in the inheritance of the saints in the kingdom of light. For he has rescued us from the dominion of darkness and brought us into the kingdom of the Son he loves, in whom we have redemption, the forgiveness of sins.

COLOSSIANS 1:12–14

Blessed are they
  whose transgressions are forgiven,
  whose sins are covered.

Blessed is the man
  whose sin the Lord will never count
  against him.

ROMANS 4:7–8

Forgiveness

I acknowledged my sin to you
  and did not cover up my iniquity.
I said, "I will confess
  my transgressions to the LORD"—
and you forgave
  the guilt of my sin.

PSALM 32:5

Let us draw near to God with a sincere heart
in full assurance of faith, having our hearts
sprinkled to cleanse us from a guilty
conscience and having our bodies washed
with pure water.

HEBREWS 10:22

Jesus is able to save completely those who
come to God through him, because he always
lives to intercede for them. Such a high priest
meets our need—one who is holy, blameless,
pure, set apart from sinners, exalted above
the heavens. Unlike the other high priests, he
does not need to offer sacrifices day after
day, first for his own sins, and then for the
sins of the people. He sacrificed for their sins
once for all when he offered himself.

HEBREWS 7:25–27

There is something God wants more than retribution. There is something he desires more than simply being paid back for the disrespect shown him. God wants fellowship with us. And he was willing to put his own system of justice on hold while he made provision for sinful men and women to be rescued.

The big picture is simply this. People turned their backs on God and God immediately went to work to regain fellowship. Observations from the Old Testament should be enough to convince us that God is a God of love and forgiveness. He forgives because he desires to forgive, not because he is under some constraint. His forgiveness is not handed out on an individual basis depending upon the sin committed. On the contrary, in the Old Testament God set up a system by which any man or woman could come to him regardless of the sin committed. In the New Testament we find that these same principles of forgiveness apply.

CHARLES STANLEY

Do not conform any longer to the pattern of this world, but be transformed by the renewing of your mind. Then you will be able to test and approve what God's will is—his good, pleasing and perfect will.

ROMANS 12:2

Teach me to do your will,
  for you are my God;
may your good Spirit
  lead me on level ground.

PSALM 143:10

I desire to do your will, O my God,
  your law is within my heart.

PSALM 40:8

Jesus said, "Whoever does the will of my Father in heaven is my brother and sister and mother."

MATTHEW 12:50

God's Will

The world and its desires pass away, but the man who does the will of God lives forever.

1 JOHN 2:17

Jesus said, "I have come down from heaven not to do my will but to do the will of him who sent me. And this is the will of him who sent me, that I shall lose none of all that he has given me, but raise them up at the last day. For my Father's will is that everyone who looks to the Son and believes in him shall have eternal life, and I will raise him up at the last day."

JOHN 6:38–40

Be joyful always; pray continually; give thanks in all circumstances, for this is God's will for you in Christ Jesus.

1 THESSALONIANS 5:16–18

God who searches our hearts knows the mind of the Spirit, because the Spirit intercedes for the saints in accordance with God's will.

ROMANS 8:27

God's Words of Life on
God's Will

This is the confidence we have in approaching God: that if we ask anything according to his will, he hears us. And if we know that he hears us—whatever we ask—we know that we have what we asked of him.

1 JOHN 5:14–15

It is God who works in you to will and to act according to his good purpose.

PHILIPPIANS 2:13

May the God of peace … equip you with everything good for doing his will, and may he work in us what is pleasing to him, through Jesus Christ, to whom be glory for ever and ever. Amen.

HEBREWS 13:20–21

I cry out to God Most High, to God,
  who fulfills his purpose for me.

PSALM 57:2

In Romans 9:16–21 Paul says that just as the potter has power over the clay so God molds us and makes us and holds us in his hand. He brings into being that which was not. He can stoop down in the dust of the earth and pick up lumps of clay and breathe the breath of life into it until it walks and talks like a natural man. The Potter has creative power.

But more, the Potter has re-creative power. Jeremiah says that sometimes the pot is marred in the potter's hand (Jeremiah 18:1–4). Sometimes the pot does not do what it was designed to do. But the potter just takes it and breaks it and molds it and makes it what he would have it to be. I'm glad to know that when I'm marred and broken, the Lord is not through with me yet. I want him to re-create me into the form of his will. Hallelujah, I am in his hand.

H. BEECHER HICKS

God's Words of Life on
Grace

It is by grace you have been saved, through faith—and this not from yourselves, it is the gift of God.

EPHESIANS 2:8

God demonstrates his own love for us in this: While we were still sinners, Christ died for us.

ROMANS 5:8

We believe it is through the grace of our Lord Jesus that we are saved.

ACTS 15:11

All have sinned and fall short of the glory of God, and are justified freely by his grace through the redemption that came by Christ Jesus.

ROMANS 3:23–24

The grace of God that brings salvation has appeared to all men.

TITUS 2:11

Grace

When the kindness and love of God our Savior appeared, he saved us, not because of righteous things we had done, but because of his mercy. He saved us through the washing of rebirth and renewal by the Holy Spirit, whom he poured out on us generously through Jesus Christ our Savior, so that, having been justified by his grace, we might become heirs having the hope of eternal life.

TITUS 3:4–7

Because of his great love for us, God, who is rich in mercy, made us alive with Christ even when we were dead in transgressions—it is by grace you have been saved.

EPHESIANS 2:4–5

Now this is our boast: Our conscience testifies that we have conducted ourselves in the world, ... in the holiness and sincerity that are from God. We have done so not according to worldly wisdom but according to God's grace.

2 CORINTHIANS 1:12

The LORD your God is gracious and compassionate. He will not turn his face from you if you return to him.

2 CHRONICLES 30:9

God opposes the proud, but gives grace to the humble.

1 PETER 5:5

The LORD longs to be gracious to you;
  he rises to show you compassion.
For the LORD is a God of justice.
  Blessed are all who wait for him!

ISAIAH 30:18

The Word became flesh and made his dwelling among us. We have seen his glory, the glory of the One and Only, who came from the Father, full of grace and truth. ... From the fullness of his grace we have all received one blessing after another. For the law was given through Moses; grace and truth came through Jesus Christ.

JOHN 1:14, 16–17

God's Words of Life on

Grace

The LORD is compassionate and gracious,
  slow to anger, abounding in love.
He will not always accuse,
  nor will he harbor his anger forever;
he does not treat us as our sins deserve
  or repay us according to our iniquities.
For as high as the heavens are above the
  earth,
  so great is his love for those who fear him;
  as far as the east is from the west,
  so far has he removed our transgressions
  from us.
As a father has compassion on his children,
  so the LORD has compassion
  on those who fear him;
for he knows how we are formed,
  he remembers that we are dust.

PSALM 103:8–14

O LORD, be gracious to us;
  we long for you.
Be our strength every morning,
  our salvation in time of distress.

ISAIAH 33:2

Grace

Since we have been justified through faith, we have peace with God through our Lord Jesus Christ, through whom we have gained access by faith into this grace in which we now stand. And we rejoice in the hope of the glory of God.

ROMANS 5:1-2

If the many died by the trespass of the one man, how much more did God's grace and the gift that came by the grace of the one man, Jesus Christ, overflow to the many! Again, the gift of God is not like the result of the one man's sin: The judgment followed one sin and brought condemnation, but the gift followed many trespasses and brought justification. For if, by the trespass of the one man, death reigned through that one man, how much more will those who receive God's abundant provision of grace and of the gift of righteousness reign in life through the one man, Jesus Christ. Consequently, just as the result of one trespass was condemnation for all men, so also the result of one act of righteousness was justification that brings life for all men.

ROMANS 5:15-18

Cheap grace is the grace we bestow on ourselves. Cheap grace is grace without discipleship, grace without the cross, grace without Jesus Christ, living and incarnate.

Costly grace is the gospel which must be sought again and again, the gift which must be asked for, the door at which a man must knock.

Such grace is costly because it calls us to follow, and it is grace because it calls us to follow Jesus Christ. It is costly because it gives a man the only true life. It is costly because it condemns sin, and grace because it justifies the sinner. Above all, it is costly because it cost God the life of his Son, and what has cost God much cannot be cheap for us. Above all, it is grace because God did not reckon his Son too dear a price to pay for our life, but delivered him up for us. Costly grace is the Incarnation of God.

DIETRICH BONHOEFFER

Devotional Thought on
Grace

Jesus said, "In my Father's house are many rooms; if it were not so, I would have told you. I am going there to prepare a place for you. And if I go and prepare a place for you, I will come back and take you to be with me that you also may be where I am."

JOHN 14:2–3

Now we know that if the earthly tent we live in is destroyed, we have a building from God, an eternal house in heaven, not built by human hands.

2 CORINTHIANS 5:1

In keeping with God's promise we are looking forward to a new heaven and a new earth, the home of righteousness.

2 PETER 3:13

Provide purses for yourselves that will not wear out, a treasure in heaven that will not be exhausted, where no thief comes near and no moth destroys. For where your treasure is, there your heart will be also.

LUKE 12:33–34

Heaven

Our light and momentary troubles are achieving for us an eternal glory that far outweighs them all.

2 CORINTHIANS 4:17

I looked and there before me was a great multitude that no one could count, from every nation, tribe, people and language, standing before the throne and in front of the Lamb. They were wearing white robes and were holding palm branches in their hands.

REVELATION 7:9

[The angel] showed me the Holy City, Jerusalem, coming down out of heaven from God. ... There will be no more night [in the Holy City]. They will not need the light of a lamp or the light of the sun, for the Lord God will give them light. And they will reign for ever and ever.

REVELATION 21:10; 22:5

God's Words of Life on
Heaven

You guide me with your counsel,
  and afterward you will take me into glory,
  O Lord.
Whom have I in heaven but you?
  And earth has nothing I desire besides you.

PSALM 73:24–25

I saw a new heaven and a new earth, for the
first heaven and the first earth had passed
away, and there was no longer any sea. I saw
the Holy City, the new Jerusalem, coming
down out of heaven from God, prepared as a
bride beautifully dressed for her husband. And
I heard a loud voice from the throne saying,
"Now the dwelling of God is with men, and he
will live with them. They will be his people, and
God himself will be with them and be their
God. He will wipe every tear from their eyes.
There will be no more death or mourning or
crying or pain, for the old order of things has
passed away."

REVELATION 21:1–4

On June 18, 1991, Dave Dravecky underwent surgery that would result in the amputation of his cancer-filled left arm. The day after surgery Dravecky looked in the mirror and reflected on the peace the Lord had given him, a peace he would soon share with another family.

A couple of days after my surgery when I was walking around, pushing my IV, I came to the visitors' room down the hall. An entire family was huddled there, sitting, waiting, paging mindlessly through last month's magazines on the coffee table. I sat down next to the mother. Her husband had cancer throughout his body and the prognosis wasn't good. You could tell they were taking it hard.

As we talked, the woman said, "My husband has never done anything bad. He's worked hard, been a good husband, a good father—yet he's in here with cancer while all sorts of bad people are out on the streets, healthy." It's hard to understand the suffering in this life, I told her, but this much I know: You can't blame God for it. Sooner or later our life on this earth is going to pass. Even the best lives someday come to an end. The only thing that will matter then is whether or not we'll get to heaven. I believe in miracles, that God can and does heal people, but more important than that, I believe in the eternal hope of heaven. When I die, that's where I'm going, because heaven is my home.

DAVE DRAVECKY

I saw the Lord seated on a throne, high and exalted, and the train of his robe filled the temple. Above him were seraphs, each with six wings: With two wings they covered their faces, with two they covered their feet, and with two they were flying. And they were calling to one another: "Holy, holy, holy is the LORD Almighty; the whole earth is full of his glory." At the sound of their voices the doorposts and thresholds shook and the temple was filled with smoke. "Woe to me!" I cried. "I am ruined! For I am a man of unclean lips, and I live among a people of unclean lips, and my eyes have seen the King, the LORD Almighty." Then one of the seraphs flew to me with a live coal in his hand, which he had taken with tongs from the altar. With it he touched my mouth and said, "See, this has touched your lips; your guilt is taken away and your sin atoned for."

ISAIAH 6:1–7

In view of God's mercy, ... offer your bodies as living sacrifices, holy and pleasing to God—this is your spiritual act of worship.

ROMANS 12:1

You were taught, with regard to your former way of life, to put off your old self, ... to be made new in the attitude of your minds; and to put on the new self, created to be like God in true righteousness and holiness.

EPHESIANS 4:22–24

Exalt the LORD our God and worship at his holy mountain,
  for the LORD our God is holy.

PSALM 99:9

As you come to him, the living Stone—rejected by men but chosen by God and precious to him—you also, like living stones, are being built into a spiritual house to be a holy priesthood, offering spiritual sacrifices acceptable to God through Jesus Christ. For in Scripture it says:
"See, I lay a stone in Zion,
  a chosen and precious cornerstone,
and the one who trusts in him
  will never be put to shame."

1 PETER 2:4–6

Who will not fear you, O Lord,
  and bring glory to your name?
For you alone are holy.
All nations will come
  and worship before you,
for your righteous acts have been revealed.

REVELATION 15:4

You are a chosen people, a royal priesthood,
a holy nation, a people belonging to God, that
you may declare the praises of him who called
you out of darkness into his wonderful light.

1 PETER 2:9

May the Lord strengthen your hearts so that
you will be blameless and holy in the presence
of our God and Father when our Lord Jesus
comes with all his holy ones.

1 THESSALONIANS 3:13

All of us who have been baptized in Christ and have "put on Christ" as a new identity are bound to be holy as he is holy. We are bound to live worthy lives, and our actions should bear witness to our union with him. He should manifest his presence in us and through us. We are supposed to be the light of the world. We are supposed to be a light to ourselves and to others. That may well be what accounts for the fact that the world is in darkness! What then is meant by the light of Christ in our lives? What is "Holiness"? What is divine sonship? Are we really seriously supposed to be saints? Can a man even desire such a thing without making a complete fool of himself in the eyes of everyone else? Is it not presumptuous? Is such a thing even possible at all? To tell the truth, many laypeople and even a good many religions do not believe, in practice, that sanctity is possible for them. Is this just plain common sense? Is it perhaps humility? Or is it defection, defeatism and despair?

If we are called by God to holiness of life and if holiness is beyond our natural power to achieve (which it certainly is) then it follows that God himself must give us the light, the strength and the courage to fulfill the task he requires of us. He will certainly give us the grace we need.

THOMAS MERTON

Devotional Thought on
Holiness

God has combined the members of the body and has given greater honor to the parts that lacked it, so that there should be no division in the body, but that its parts should have equal concern for each other. If one part suffers, every part suffers with it; if one part is honored, every part rejoices with it.

1 CORINTHIANS 12:24–26

Honor the LORD with your wealth.

PROVERBS 3:9

He who speaks on his own does so to gain honor for himself, but he who works for the honor of the one who sent him is a man of truth; there is nothing false about him.

JOHN 7:18

Do you not know that your body is a temple of the Holy Spirit, who is in you, whom you have received from God? You are not your own; you were bought at a price. Therefore honor God with your body.

1 CORINTHIANS 6:19–20

A man's pride brings him low,
  but a man of lowly spirit gains honor.

PROVERBS 29:23

What is man that you are mindful of him,
  the son of man that you care for him?
You made him a little lower than the heavenly
  beings and crowned him with glory and
  honor, O LORD.

PSALM 8:4–5

Wealth and honor come from you, Lord;
  you are the ruler of all things.

1 CHRONICLES 29:12

Be devoted to one another in brotherly love.
Honor one another above yourselves.

ROMANS 12:10

God "will give to each person according to
what he has done." To those who by persis-
tence in doing good seek glory, honor and
immortality, he will give eternal life.

ROMANS 2:6–7

Jesus said, "Whoever serves me must follow me; and where I am, my servant also will be. My Father will honor the one who serves me."

JOHN 12:26

God alone is my rock and my salvation;
  he is my fortress, I will not be shaken.
My salvation and my honor depend on God;
  he is my mighty rock, my refuge.

PSALM 62:6–7

You will increase my honor
  and comfort me once again, O LORD.

PSALM 71:21

The LORD God is a sun and shield;
  the LORD bestows favor and honor;
no good thing does he withhold
  from those whose walk is blameless.

PSALM 84:11

When Jesus was asked to name the great commandments in the Scriptures, he didn't hesitate in the least. He told a young lawyer, "Love the Lord you God with all your heart and with all your soul and with all your mind … Love your neighbor as yourself" (Matthew 22:37, 39). Loving God, loving others and finding value in ourselves. Without a doubt, these three aspects of love are the most effective weapons against the destructive power of low self-worth.

Genuine love is a gift we give others. It isn't purchased by their actions or contingent upon our emotions at the moment. It may carry with it strong emotional feelings, but it isn't supported by them. Rather, it is a decision we make on a daily basis that someone is special and valuable to us.

Like genuine love, honor is a gift we give to someone. It involves the decision we make before we put love into action that a person is of high value. In fact, love for someone often begins to flow once we have made the decision to honor him or her.

GARY SMALLEY AND JOHN TRENT

Devotional Thought on

Honor

God's Words of Life on

Hope

We know that in all things God works for the good of those who love him, who have been called according to his purpose. ... What, then, shall we say in response to this? If God is for us, who can be against us?

ROMANS 8:28, 31

Even youths grow tired and weary,
  and young men stumble and fall;
but those who hope in the LORD
  will renew their strength.
They will soar on wings like eagles;
  they will run and not grow weary,
  they will walk and not be faint.

ISAIAH 40:30–31

Let us hold unswervingly to the hope we profess, for God who promised is faithful.

HEBREWS 10:23

You will know that I am the LORD;
  those who hope in me will not be
  disappointed.

ISAIAH 49:23

Hope that is seen is no hope at all. Who hopes for what he already has? But if we hope for what we do not yet have, we wait for it patiently.

ROMANS 8:24–25

We wait in hope for the LORD;
 he is our help and our shield.
In him our hearts rejoice,
 for we trust in his holy name.
May your unfailing love rest upon us, O LORD,
 even as we put our hope in you.

PSALM 33:20–22

Everything is possible for him who believes.

MARK 9:23

"I will ransom [my people] from the power of
 the grave;
I will redeem them from death.
Where, O death, are your plagues?
 Where, O grave, is your destruction?"
 says the LORD.

HOSEA 13:14

I consider that our present sufferings are not worth comparing with the glory that will be revealed in us.

ROMANS 8:18

I pray ... that the eyes of your heart may be enlightened in order that you may know the hope to which God has called you, the riches of his glorious inheritance in the saints, and his incomparable great power for us who believe.

EPHESIANS 1:18-19

Because God wanted to make the unchanging nature of his purpose very clear to the heirs of what was promised, he confirmed it with an oath. God did this so that, by two unchangeable things in which it is impossible for God to lie, we who have fled to take hold of the hope offered to us may be greatly encouraged. We have this hope as an anchor for the soul, firm and secure.

HEBREWS 6:17-19

When the kindness and love of God our Savior
appeared, he saved us, not because of righteous things we had done, but because of his
mercy. He saved us through the washing of
rebirth and renewal by the Holy Spirit, whom
he poured out on us generously through
Jesus Christ our Savior, so that, having been
justified by his grace, we might become heirs
having the hope of eternal life.

TITUS 3:4–7

Dear friends, now we are children of God, and
what we will be has not yet been made
known. But we know that when Christ
appears, we shall be like him, for we shall see
him as he is. Everyone who has this hope in
him purifies himself, just as he is pure.

1 JOHN 3:2–3

Through Christ you believe in God, who raised
him from the dead and glorified him, and so
your faith and hope are in God.

1 PETER 1:21

Hope

Praise be to the God and Father of our Lord Jesus Christ! In his great mercy he has given us new birth into a living hope through the resurrection of Jesus Christ from the dead, and into an inheritance that can never perish, spoil or fade—kept in heaven for you, who through faith are shielded by God's power until the coming of the salvation that is ready to be revealed in the last time.

1 PETER 1:3-5

"I know the plans I have for you," declares the LORD, "plans to prosper you and not to harm you, plans to give you hope and a future."

JEREMIAH 29:11

May our Lord Jesus Christ himself and God our Father, who loved us and by his grace gave us eternal encouragement and good hope, encourage your hearts and strengthen you in every good deed and word.

2 THESSALONIANS 2:16-17

God's Words of Life on

Hope

Why are you downcast, O my soul?
Why so disturbed within me?
Put your hope in God,
  for I will yet praise him,
  my Savior and my God.

PSALM 42:11

This is a trustworthy saying that deserves full
acceptance (and for this we labor and strive),
that we have put our hope in the living God,
who is the Savior of all men, and especially of
those who believe.

1 TIMOTHY 4:9–10

The grace of God that brings salvation has
appeared to all men. It teaches us to say "No"
to ungodliness and worldly passions, and to
live self-controlled, upright and godly lives in
this present age, while we wait for the
blessed hope—the glorious appearing of our
great God and Savior, Jesus Christ, who gave
himself for us to redeem us from all wicked-
ness and to purify for himself a people that
are his very own, eager to do what is good.

TITUS 2:11–14

Hope

God has delivered us from such a deadly peril, and he will deliver us. On him we have set our hope that he will continue to deliver us.

2 CORINTHIANS 1:10

If only for this life we have hope in Christ, we are to be pitied more than all men. But Christ has indeed been raised from the dead, the firstfruits of those who have fallen asleep. For since death came through a man, the resurrection of the dead comes also through a man. For as in Adam all die, so in Christ all will be made alive.

1 CORINTHIANS 15:19–22

May the God of hope fill you with all joy and peace as you trust in him, so that you may overflow with hope by the power of the Holy Spirit.

ROMANS 15:13

The most important lesson I've learned in my life is that God is so gracious that he accepts me, my failures, my personality quirks, my shortcomings and all.

It's hard for a perfectionist like me, but I have to admit I can never be good enough. No matter how sound my strategy, how much I study, how hard I work—I'll always be a failure when it comes to being perfect. Yet God loves me anyway. And believing that gives me the greatest sense of peace, hope and security in the world.

It's that belief, that faith, more than anything else, that enabled me to last twenty-nine years on the sidelines of the Dallas Cowboys. And it's that faith that gives me hope for whatever the future holds for me outside of professional football.

TOM LANDRY

God's Words of Life on
Identity

The LORD your God is with you.
  he is mighty to save.
He will take great delight in you,
  he will quiet you with his love
  he will rejoice over you with singing.

ZEPHANIAH 3:17

If we live, we live to the Lord; and if we die, we die to the Lord. So, whether we live or die, we belong to the Lord.

ROMANS 14:8

How great is the love the Father has lavished on us, that we should be called children of God! And that is what we are!

1 JOHN 3:1

"See, I have engraved you on the palms of my hands," says the LORD.

ISAIAH 49:16

God's Words of Life on
Identity

Jesus said, "Are not five sparrows sold for two pennies? Yet not one of them is forgotten by God. Indeed, the very hairs of your head are all numbered. Don't be afraid; you are worth more than many sparrows."

LUKE 12:6–7

You created my inmost being;
  you knit me together in my mother's womb.
I praise you because I am fearfully
  and wonderfully made;
  your works are wonderful,
  I know that full well.

PSALM 139:13–14

Know that the LORD is God.
  It is he who made us, and we are his;
  we are his people, the sheep of his pasture.
Enter his gates with thanksgiving
  and his courts with praise;
  give thanks to him and praise his name.
For the LORD is good and his love endures
  forever; his faithfulness continues
  through all generations.

PSALM 100:3-5

Jesus said, "I am the vine; you are the branches. If a man remains in me and I in him, he will bear much fruit; apart from me you can do nothing. ... This is to my Father's glory, that you bear much fruit, showing yourselves to be my disciples."

JOHN 15:5, 8

So God created man in his own image, in the image of God he created him; male and female he created them.

GENESIS 1:27

"I will be a Father to you,
   and you will be my sons and daughters,"
      says the Lord Almighty.

2 CORINTHIANS 6:18

We are God's workmanship, created in Christ Jesus to do good works, which God prepared in advance for us to do.

EPHESIANS 2:10

God's Words of Life on
Identity

What is man that you are mindful of him,
  O LORD, the son of man that you
  care for him?
You made him a little lower than the heavenly
  beings and crowned him with
  glory and honor.
You made him ruler over the works
  of your hands;
  you put everything under his feet.

PSALM 8:4–6

The Spirit himself testifies with our spirit that
we are God's children. Now if we are children,
then we are heirs—heirs of God and co-heirs
with Christ, if indeed we share in his sufferings in order that we may also share
in his glory.

ROMANS 8:16–17

We are the temple of the living God. As God
has said: "I will live with them and walk among
them, and I will be their God, and they will be
my people."

2 CORINTHIANS 6:16

When Christ, who is your life, appears, then
you also will appear with him in glory.

COLOSSIANS 3:4

Identity

"Fear not, for I have redeemed you;
  I have summoned you by name; you are
  mine," says the LORD.

ISAIAH 43:1

In God we live and move and have our being.

ACTS 17:28

"I know the plans I have for you," declares the
LORD, "plans to prosper you and not to harm
you, plans to give you hope and a future. Then
you will call upon me and come and pray to
me, and I will listen to you. You will seek me
and find me when you seek me with all your
heart. I will be found by you," declares
the LORD.

JEREMIAH 29:11–14

You have been born again, not of perishable
seed, but of imperishable, through the living
and enduring word of God.

1 PETER 1:23

A man's identity is based on who he is apart from what he does. Identity is a matter of character, not accomplishment, a matter of being and relating, not doing. This is apparent in the call of Jesus Christ to his disciples. Notice that Jesus definitely called the apostles to do something: to preach the gospel and drive out demons. But his first call was for them to be someone—his men. He wanted a mutually loving, nurturing, caring relationship with these men.

Christ's acceptance and approval of his disciples was always based on the being part of discipleship, not the doing part. The disciples enjoyed some successes in their mission. But they also experienced some failures, particularly during Christ's arrest, trial and crucifixion. Had the disciples based their identity on their performance, they would have reason to consider themselves failures. But after his resurrection, Jesus gave them the Great Commission and the disciples successfully carried it out because they had a firm grasp on their identity in Christ.

STEPHEN ARTERBURN AND DAVID STOOP

Devotional Thought on

Identity

God's Words of Life on
Integrity

Let us not become weary in doing good, for at the proper time we will reap a harvest if we do not give up.

GALATIANS 6:9

You need to persevere so that when you have done the will of God, you will receive what he has promised.

HEBREWS 10:36

Let love and faithfulness never leave you;
  bind them around your neck,
  write them on the tablet of your heart.
Then you will win favor and a good name
  in the sight of God and man.

PROVERBS 3:3–4

The integrity of the upright guides them.

PROVERBS 11:3

Integrity

The man of integrity walks securely,
   but he who takes crooked paths will
      be found out.

PROVERBS 10:9

I know, my God, that you test the heart and
are pleased with integrity.

1 CHRONICLES 29:17

May integrity and uprightness protect me,
   because my hope is in you, O LORD.

PSALM 25:21

I know that you are pleased with me, LORD,
   for my enemy does not triumph over me.
In my integrity you uphold me
   and set me in your presence forever.

PSALM 41:11–12

Righteousness guards the man of integrity.

PROVERBS 13:6

May the words of my mouth and
the meditation of my heart
be pleasing in your sight,
O LORD, my Rock and my Redeemer.

PSALM 19:14

LORD, who may dwell in your sanctuary?
Who may live on your holy hill?
He whose walk is blameless
and who does what is righteous,
who speaks the truth from his heart.

PSALM 15:1–2

Search me, O God, and know my heart;
test me and know my anxious thoughts.
See if there is any offensive way in me,
and lead me in the way everlasting.

PSALM 139:23–24

Lord, make me an
instrument of your peace!
Where there is hatred,
let me sow love;
where there is injury, pardon;
where there is doubt, faith;
where there is despair, hope;
where there is darkness, light;
and where there is sadness, joy.

O Divine Master,
grant that I may not
So much seek to be consoled
as to console;
to be understood
as to understand;
to be loved
as to love;
for it is in giving
that we receive;
it is in pardoning
that we are pardoned;
and it is in dying
that we are born to Eternal Life.

ST. FRANCIS OF ASSISI

Devotional Thought on

Integrity

God's Words of Life on

Joy

Though you have not seen Jesus, you love him; and even though you do not see him now, you believe in him and are filled with an inexpressible and glorious joy, for you are receiving the goal of your faith, the salvation of your souls.

1 PETER 1:8–9

Shout for joy to the LORD, all the earth. Worship the LORD with gladness;
  come before him with joyful songs.

PSALM 100:1–2

Do not grieve, for the joy of the LORD is your strength.

NEHEMIAH 8:10

Satisfy us in the morning with your unfailing love, O LORD,
  that we may sing for joy and be glad
  all our days.

PSALM 90:14

May the God of hope fill you with all joy and peace as you trust in him, so that you may overflow with hope by the power of the Holy Spirit.

ROMANS 15:13

Joy

A cheerful look brings joy to the heart,
  and good news gives health to the bones.

PROVERBS 15:30

Jesus said, "As the Father has loved me, so
have I loved you. Now remain in my love. If
you obey my commands, you will remain in my
love, just as I have obeyed my Father's commands and remain in his love. I have told you
this so that my joy may be in you and that
your joy may be complete."

JOHN 15:9–11

You have made known to me the path of life,
  O Lord;
  you will fill me with joy in your presence,
  with eternal pleasures at your right hand.

PSALM 16:11

Weeping may remain for a night,
  but rejoicing comes in the morning.

PSALM 30:5

God's Words of Life on
Joy

Those who sow in tears
  will reap with songs of joy.

PSALM 126:5

The ransomed of the LORD will return.
They will enter Zion with singing;
  everlasting joy will crown their heads.
Gladness and joy will overtake them,
  and sorrow and sighing will flee away.

ISAIAH 35:10

The kingdom of God is not a matter of eating
and drinking, but of righteousness, peace and
joy in the Holy Spirit.

ROMANS 14:17

Our mouths were filled with laughter,
  our tongues with songs of joy.
Then it was said among the nations,
  "The LORD has done great things for them."
The LORD has done great things for us,
  and we are filled with joy.

PSALM 126:2–3

Let all who take refuge in you be glad;
  let them ever sing for joy.
Spread your protection over them,
  that those who love your name may rejoice
    in you.
For surely, O LORD, you bless the righteous;
  you surround them with your favor
    as with a shield.

PSALM 5:11–12

The LORD is my strength and my shield;
  my heart trusts in him, and I am helped.
My heart leaps for joy
  and I will give thanks to him in song.

PSALM 28:7

You turned my wailing into dancing;
  you removed my sackcloth and clothed me
    with joy,
that my heart may sing to you and
  not be silent.

O LORD my God, I will give you thanks forever.

PSALM 30:11–12

God's Words of Life on
Joy

Those living far away fear your wonders,
 O LORD;
 where morning dawns and evening fades
 you call forth songs of joy.

PSALM 65:8

When I said, "My foot is slipping,"
 your love, O LORD, supported me.
When anxiety was great within me,
 your consolation brought joy to my soul.

PSALM 94:18–19

Light is shed upon the righteous
 and joy on the upright in heart.

PSALM 97:11

To God who is able to keep you from falling
and to present you before his glorious presence without fault and with great joy—to the
only God our Savior be glory, majesty, power
and authority, through Jesus Christ our Lord,
before all ages, now and forevermore! Amen.

JUDE 24–25

No summary of the prophets would be complete apart from one last message: their loud insistence that the world will not end in "universal final defeat," but in Joy. Their voices soar like songbirds' when the prophets turn at last to describe the Joy beyond the walls of the world. In that final day, God will roll up the earth like a carpet and weave it anew. There will be no fear then, and no pain. No infants will die; no tears will fall. Among the nations, peace will flow like a river and armies will melt their weapons into farm tools. No one will complain about the hiddenness of God in that day. His glory will fill the earth, and the sun will seem dim by contrast.

Human history is not an end in itself but a transition time, a parenthesis between Eden and the new heaven and new earth still to be formed by God. Even when everything seems out of control, God is firmly in control, and someday will assert himself.

PHILIP YANCEY

Devotional Thought on Joy

God's Words of Life on
Leadership

You guide me with your counsel, LORD,
  and afterward you will take me into glory.

PSALM 73:24

We have different gifts, according to the
grace given us. If a man's gift is prophesying,
let him use it in proportion to his faith. If it is
serving, let him serve; if it is teaching, let him
teach; if it is encouraging, let him encourage,
if it is contributing to the needs of others, let
him give generously; if it is leadership, let him
govern diligently, if it is showing mercy, let him
do it cheerfully.

ROMANS 12:6–8

The LORD will guide you always;
  he will satisfy your needs
in a sun-scorched land
  and will strengthen your frame.
You will be like a well-watered garden,
  like a spring whose waters never fail.

ISAIAH 58:11

The LORD is my shepherd,
I shall not be in want.
He makes me lie down in green pastures,
  he leads me beside quiet waters,
  he restores my soul.
He guides me in paths of righteousness
  for his name's sake.

PSALM 23:1–3

"I will give you shepherds after my own heart,
who will lead you with knowledge and understanding," says the LORD.

JEREMIAH 3:15

Keep watch over yourselves and all the flock
of which the Holy Spirit has made you overseers. Be shepherds of the church of God,
which he bought with his own blood.

ACTS 20:28

Jesus said, "I have set you an example that
you should do as I have done for you. I tell you
the truth, no servant is greater than his
master, nor is a messenger greater than the
one who sent him. Now that you know these
things, you will blessed if you do them."

JOHN 13:15–17

Leadership

Thanks be to God, who always leads us in triumphal procession in Christ and through us spreads everywhere the fragrance of the knowledge of him.

2 CORINTHIANS 2:14

Those who are led by the Spirit of God are sons of God.

ROMANS 8:14

Be shepherds of God's flock that is under your care, serving as overseers—not because you must, but because you are willing, as God wants you to be; not greedy for money, but eager to serve; not lording it over those entrusted to you, but being examples to the flock. And when the Chief Shepherd appears, you will receive the crown of glory that will never fade away.

1 PETER 5:2–4

Those who are wise will shine like the brightness of the heavens, and those who lead many to righteousness, like the stars for ever and ever.

DANIEL 12:3

If you were to travel into the future, what would your legacy look like? Would there be a chain linking generation to generation with godly men and women who in turn produced more godly men and women?

The destiny of those future generations is in your hands. The choices you make with your family, and the others you lead, today, will determine the quality of life in your family tree, and that of others, for generations to come. That's why one man can make a difference. So the question is, how are we going to do that? My sons are still young. I've still got a few years before they head off to college, but that time will simply fly by. So I must have a pretty clear idea of what I need to teach them during those remaining years. I must ask myself: What do I specifically need to do in order to train them to become leaders of their families?

I have five goals for saving my boys. It is my job as their father to model for them the importance of:

Knowing and obeying Jesus Christ

Knowing and displaying godly character

Knowing and loving my wife

Knowing and loving my children

Knowing my gifts and abilities so I can work hard and effectively in an area of strength

If you provide godly leadership to all that follow you now, it will be the greatest and most fulfilling task of your life.

STEVE FARRAR

God's Words of Life on

Love

I will praise you, O Lord, among the nations;
  I will sing of you among the peoples.
For great is your love,
reaching to the heavens;
  your faithfulness reaches to the skies.

PSALM 57:9–10

Jesus said, "Love one another. As I have loved you, so you must love one another. By this all men will know that you are my disciples, if you love one another."

JOHN 13:34–35

Be imitators of God as dearly loved children and live a life of love, just as Christ loved us and gave himself up for us.

EPHESIANS 5:1–2

I trust in your unfailing love, O Lord;
  my heart rejoices in your salvation.
I will sing to the Lord,
  for he has been good to me.

PSALM 13:5–6

I pray that you, being rooted and established in love, may have power, together with all the saints, to grasp how wide and long and high and deep is the love of Christ, and to know this love that surpasses knowledge—that you may be filled to the measure of all the fullness of God.

EPHESIANS 3:17–19

Love is patient, love is kind. It does not envy, it does not boast, it is not proud. It is not rude, it is not self-seeking, it is not easily angered, it keeps no record of wrongs. Love does not delight in evil but rejoices with the truth. It always protects, always trusts, always hopes, always perseveres. Love never fails.

1 CORINTHIANS 13:4–8

Greater love has no one than this, that he lay down his life for his friends.

JOHN 15:13

We know and rely on the love God has for us. God is love. Whoever lives in love lives in God, and God in him.

1 JOHN 4:16

Love and faithfulness meet together;
  righteousness and peace kiss each other.

PSALM 85:10

God's Words of Life on
Love

God has poured out his love into our hearts
by the Holy Spirit, whom he has given us. ...
God demonstrates his own love for us in this:
While we were still sinners, Christ died for us.

ROMANS 5:5, 8

God did not give us a spirit of timidity, but a
spirit of power, of love and of self-discipline.

2 TIMOTHY 1:7

He who covers over an offense
promotes love.

PROVERBS 17:9

The LORD loves righteousness and justice;
the earth is full of his unfailing love.

PSALM 33:5

There is no fear in love. But perfect love
drives out fear.

1 JOHN 4:18

Love

As God's chosen people, holy and dearly loved, clothe yourselves with compassion, kindness, humility, gentleness and patience. Bear with each other and forgive whatever grievances you may have against one another. Forgive as the Lord forgave you. And over all these virtues put on love, which binds them all together in perfect unity.

COLOSSIANS 3:12–14

Love the LORD your God with all your heart and with all your soul and with all your strength.

DEUTERONOMY 6:5

God so loved the world that he gave his one and only Son, that whoever believes in him shall not perish but have eternal life.

JOHN 3:16

Because of the LORD 's great love we are
    not consumed,
  for his compassions never fail.
They are new every morning;
  great is your faithfulness.

LAMENTATIONS 3:22–23

Love

Mercy, peace and love be yours in abundance.

JUDE 2

Grace, mercy and peace from God the Father and from Jesus Christ, the Father's Son, will be with us in truth and love.

2 JOHN 1:3

Dear friends, let us love one another, for love comes from God. Everyone who loves has been born of God and knows God.

1 JOHN 4:7

How great is the love the Father has lavished on us, that we should be called children of God! And that is what we are!

1 JOHN 3:1

Above all, love each other deeply, because love covers over a multitude of sins.

1 PETER 4:8

To believe means to realize not just with the head but also with the heart that God loves me in a creative, intimate, unique, reliable and tender way.

Creative: out of his love I came forth; through his love I am who I am.

Intimate: his love reaches out to the deepest in me.

Unique: his love embraces me as I am, not as I am considered to be by other people or supposed to be in my own self-image.

Reliable: his love will never let me down.

Tender: tenderness is what happens to you when you know you are deeply and sincerely liked by someone.

BRENNAN MANNING

More than anything else in heaven or on earth,
I pray for the power to love my fellow person, ...
And I pray as well for the ability to translate the message of God's eternal love into words that will pierce the benumbed minds of busy men
and move their hearts to faith and obedience.

LESLIE BRANDT

Devotional Thought on
Love

A patient man has great understanding,
  but a quick-tempered man displays folly.

PROVERBS 14:29

The end of a matter is better than
its beginning,
  and patience is better than pride.

ECCLESIASTES 7:8

Better a patient man than a warrior,
  a man who controls his temper
    than one who takes a city.

PROVERBS 16:32

Be patient, ... until the Lord's coming. See
how the farmer waits for the land to yield its
valuable crop and how patient he is for the
autumn and spring rains. Be patient and
stand firm, because the Lord's coming is
near.

JAMES 5:7–8

If we hope for what we do not yet have, we
wait for it patiently.

ROMANS 8:25

Patience

Love is patient.

1 CORINTHIANS 13:4

Be joyful in hope, patient in affliction,
faithful in prayer.

ROMANS 12:12

You need to persevere so that when you have
done the will of God, you will receive what he
has promised.

HEBREWS 10:36

I waited patiently for the LORD;
he turned to me and heard my cry.

PSALM 40:1

A man's wisdom gives him patience;
it is to his glory to overlook an offense.

PROVERBS 19:11

Patience

Perseverance must finish its work so that you may be mature and complete, not lacking anything.

JAMES 1:4

A hot-tempered man stirs up dissension,
  but a patient man calms a quarrel.

PROVERBS 15:18

Be still before the LORD and wait patiently
  for him;
  do not fret when men succeed in their ways,
  when they carry out their wicked schemes.

PSALM 37:7

The Lord is not slow in keeping his promise, as some understand slowness. He is patient with you, not wanting anyone to perish, but everyone to come to repentance.

2 PETER 3:9

The fruit of the Spirit is love, joy, peace, patience, kindness, goodness, faithfulness, gentleness and self-control.

GALATIANS 5:22–23

To wait on God is to struggle and sometimes to fail. Sometimes the failures teach us more than the successes. For the failures teach us that to wait on God is not only to wait for his mercy, but to wait by his mercy. The glory hidden in our failures is the discovery that the very thing we wait for is what we wait by! The success of our waiting lies not in who we are, but in who God is. It is not our strength that will pull us through to the end, it is God's amazing grace and mercy.

BEN PATTERSON

Devotional Thought on

Patience

I wait for the LORD, my soul waits,
   and in his word I put my hope.
My soul waits for the LORD
   more than watchmen wait for the morning.

PSALM 130:5–6

Peace

You will keep in perfect peace
  him whose mind is steadfast,
  because he trusts in you, O LORD.

ISAIAH 26:3

The peace of God, which transcends all
understanding, will guard your hearts and
your minds in Christ Jesus.

PHILIPPIANS 4:7

Better a dry crust with peace and quiet
  than a house full of feasting, with strife.

PROVERBS 17:1

Great peace have they who love your law,
  O LORD, and nothing can make
  them stumble.

PSALM 119:165

Let the peace of Christ rule in your hearts,
since as members of one body you were
called to peace. And be thankful.

COLOSSIANS 3:15

Peace

Aim for perfection, listen to my appeal, be of one mind, live in peace. And the God of love and peace will be with you.

2 CORINTHIANS 13:11

The fruit of righteousness will be peace;
the effect of righteousness will be quietness
and confidence forever.

ISAIAH 32:17

Jesus said, "Peace I leave with you; my peace I give you. I do not give to you as the world gives. Do not let your hearts be troubled and do not be afraid."

JOHN 14:27

The LORD bless you
and keep you;
the LORD make his face shine upon you
and be gracious to you;
the LORD turn his face toward you
and give you peace.

NUMBERS 6:24–26

God's Words of Life on
Peace

The LORD gives strength to his people;
the LORD blesses his people with peace.

PSALM 29:11

Consider the blameless, observe the upright;
there is a future for the man of peace.

PSALM 37:37

I will listen to what God the LORD will say;
he promises peace to his people, his saints.

PSALM 85:8

A heart at peace gives life to the body.

PROVERBS 14:30

I will lie down and sleep in peace,
for you alone, O LORD,
make me dwell in safety.

PSALM 4:8

There is joy for those who promote peace.

PROVERBS 12:20

When a man's ways are pleasing
  to the LORD,
he makes even his enemies live at peace
with him.

PROVERBS 16:7

To us a child is born,
  to us a son is given,
  and the government will
  be on his shoulders.
And he will be called
  Wonderful Counselor, Mighty God,
  Everlasting Father, Prince of Peace.

ISAIAH 9:6

LORD, you establish peace for us;
  all that we have accomplished
  you have done for us.

ISAIAH 26:12

Those who walk uprightly
  enter into peace.

ISAIAH 57:2

Peace

How beautiful on the mountains
  are the feet of those who bring good news,
who proclaim peace,
  who bring good tidings,
  who proclaim salvation,
who say to Zion,
  "Your God reigns!"

ISAIAH 52:7

"Though the mountains be shaken
  and the hills be removed,
yet my unfailing love for you will not be shaken
  nor my covenant of peace be removed,"
  says the LORD, who has compassion on you.

ISAIAH 54:10

Be still, and know that I am God.

PSALM 46:10

If you love excitement and enjoy the thrill of challenge, you will have to work a little harder at controlling your adrenalin—because you have a greater tendency to produce too much of it. You may have to work at learning to enjoy life without constant novel stimulation. You will have to train yourself to come down frequently from the "mountaintop" and enjoy the peace of the valley, where recuperation and healing can take place.

The accelerated pace of modern living tends to rob us of natural recovery time, so that must be planned into our lives by deliberate design. Even Jesus was aware of this need for recovery. In Mark 6:31, he told his disciples, "Come with me by yourselves to a quiet place and get some rest."

If Jesus thought it necessary for him and his disciples to rest from time to time, who are we to think we can get by without it?

ARCHIBALD HART

Prayer

In my distress I called to the LORD,
and he answered me.

JONAH 2:2

I called on your name, O LORD,
from the depths of the pit.
You heard my plea: "Do not close you ears
to my cry for relief."
You came near when I called you,
and you said, "Do not fear."

LAMENTATIONS 3:55–57

When you pray go into your room, close the
door and pray to your Father, who is unseen.
Then your Father, who sees what is done in
secret, will reward you.

MATTHEW 6:6

The LORD has heard my cry for mercy;
the LORD accepts my prayer.

PSALM 6:9

Be joyful in hope, patient in affliction,
faithful in prayer.

ROMANS 12:12

God's Words of Life on
Prayer

I urge ... that requests, prayers, intercession and thanksgiving be made for everyone—for kings and all those in authority, that we may live peaceful and quiet lives in all godliness and holiness.

1 TIMOTHY 2:1-2

"Call to me and I will answer you and tell you great and unsearchable things you do not know," says the LORD.

JEREMIAH 33:3

If any of you lacks wisdom, he should ask God, who gives generously to all without finding fault, and it will be given to him.

JAMES 1:5

O LORD, I call to you; come quickly to me.
  Hear my voice when I call to you.
May my prayer be set before you like incense;
  may the lifting up of my hands be like the
  evening sacrifice.

PSALM 141:1–2

God's Words of Life on
Prayer

The prayer offered in faith will make the sick person well; the Lord will raise him up. If he has sinned, he will be forgiven. Therefore confess your sins to each other and pray for each other so that you may be healed. The prayer of a righteous man is powerful and effective.

JAMES 5:15–16

Know that the LORD has set apart the godly
  for himself;
 the LORD will hear when I call
  to him.

PSALM 4:3

This is the confidence we have in approaching God: that if we ask anything according to his will, he hears us. And if we know that he hears us—whatever we ask—we know that we have what we asked of him.

1 JOHN 5:14–15

Hear my prayer, O LORD;
 listen to my cry for mercy.
In the day of my trouble I will call to you
 for you will answer me.

PSALM 86:6

Jesus told his disciples a parable to show them that they should always pray and not give up. He said: "In a certain town there was a judge who neither feared God nor cared about men. And there was a widow in that town who kept coming to him with the plea, 'Grant me justice against my adversary.'

"For some time he refused. But finally he said to himself, 'Even though I don't fear God or care about men, yet because this widow keeps bothering me, I will see that she gets justice, so that she won't eventually wear me out with her coming!'"

And the Lord said, "Listen to what the unjust judge says. And will not God bring about justice for his chosen ones, who cry out to him day and night? Will he keep putting them off? I tell you, he will see that they get justice, and quickly."

LUKE 18:1–8

Do not be anxious about anything, but in everything, by prayer and petition, with thanksgiving, present your requests to God. And the peace of God, which transcends all understanding, will guard your hearts and your minds in Christ Jesus.

PHILIPPIANS 4:6–7

The Spirit helps us in our weakness. We do not know what we ought to pray for, but the Spirit himself intercedes for us with groans that words cannot express.

ROMANS 8:26

The eyes of the Lord are on the righteous and his ears are attentive to their prayer.

1 PETER 3:12

In the morning, O LORD, you hear my voice;
   in the morning I lay my requests before you
   and wait in expectation.

PSALM 5:3

Prayer is one of the unlimited resources available to each of us. In this bound-up world, prayer may be a lost art, but it is always the starting point when we move toward God. In prayer we set aside our agendas, letting God's priorities become our priorities, and we receive his resources.

JOHN F. WESTFALL

You don't have to learn some special prayer jargon to start a conversation with God. Honesty and a willingness to establish a personal relationship with him are the only initial requirements. God is looking for an opportunity to reveal himself to you, so if you put him to the test and then watch for an answer without too many preconceptions about how that answer will come, I can guarantee you that you'll be in for some exciting surprises.

PAT BOONE

God is not far from each one of us.

ACTS 17:27

Come near to God and he will come
near to you.

JAMES 4:8

Where can I go from your Spirit?
  Where can I flee from your presence?
If I go up to the heavens, you are there;
  if I make my bed in the depths,
  you are there.
If I rise on the wings of the dawn,
  if I settle on the far side of the sea,
even there your hand will guide me,
  your right hand will hold me fast.

PSALM 139:7–10

The LORD searches every heart and understands every motive behind the thoughts. If
you seek him, he will be found by you.

1 CHRONICLES 28:9

"I am with you and will watch over you wherever you go. ... I will not leave you until I have done what I have promised you," says the LORD.

GENESIS 28:15

The LORD is with you when you are with him.

2 CHRONICLES 15:2

From birth I was cast upon you;
  from my mother's womb you have been
  my God.
Do not be far from me,
  for trouble is near
  and there is no one to help. ...
But you, O LORD, be not far off;
  O my Strength, come quickly to help me.

PSALM 22:10–11, 19

No one has ever seen God; but if we love one another, God lives in us and his love is made complete in us.

1 JOHN 4:12

God has said,
"Never will I leave you;
never will I forsake you."

HEBREWS 13:5

I am convinced that neither death nor life, neither angels nor demons, neither the present nor the future, nor any powers, neither height nor depth, nor anything else in all creation, will be able to separate us from the love of God that is in Christ Jesus our Lord.

ROMANS 8:38–39

I heard a loud voice from the throne saying, "Now the dwelling of God is with men, and he will live with them. They will be his people, and God himself will be with them and be their God."

REVELATION 21:3

Jesus said, "I will ask the Father, and he will give you another Counselor to be with you forever."

JOHN 14:16

What we need to know, of course, is not just that God exists, not just that beyond the steely brightness of the stars there is a cosmic intelligence of some kind that keeps the whole show going, but that there is a God right here in the thick of our day-by-day lives who may not be writing messages about himself in the stars, but in one way or another, is trying to get messages through our blindness as we move around here knee-deep in the fragrant muck and misery and marvel of the world. It is not objective proof of God's existence that we want but that experience of God's presence. That is the miracle we are really after, and that is also, I think, the miracle that we really get.

FREDERICK BUECHNER

Devotional Thought on
Presence of God

Priorities

We pray that you may live a life worthy of the Lord and may please him in every way: bearing fruit in every good work, growing in the knowledge of God.

COLOSSIANS 1:10

Do not wear yourself out to get rich;
  have the wisdom to show restraint.

PROVERBS 23:4

This is what the LORD says:
"Let not the wise man boast of his wisdom
  or the strong man boast of his strength
  or the rich man boast of his riches,
but let him who boasts boast about this:
  that he understands and knows me,
that I am the LORD, who exercises kindness,
  justice and righteousness on earth,
  for in these I delight."

JEREMIAH 9:23–24

Choose for yourselves this day whom you will serve. ... But as for me and my household, we will serve the LORD.

JOSHUA 24:15

Priorities

Jesus said, "Do not worry, saying 'What shall we eat?' or 'What shall we drink?' or 'What shall we wear?' For ... your heavenly Father knows that you need them. But seek first his kingdom and his righteousness, and all these things will be given to you as well."

MATTHEW 6:31–33

What does the LORD require of you?
To act justly and to love mercy
    and to walk humbly with your God.

MICAH 6:8

Whatever is true, whatever is noble, whatever is right, whatever is pure, whatever is lovely, whatever is admirable—if anything is excellent or praiseworthy—think about such things.

PHILIPPIANS 4:8

Give everyone what you owe him: If you owe taxes, pay taxes; if revenue, then revenue; if respect, then respect; if honor, then honor. Let no debt remain outstanding, except the continuing debt to love one another, for he who loves his fellowman has fulfilled the law.

ROMANS 13:7–8

God's Words of Life on
Priorities

The LORD appeared to Solomon during the night in a dream, and God said, "Ask for whatever you want me to give you." …

[Solomon answered,] "Now, O LORD my God, you have made your servant king in place of my father David. But I am only a little child and do not know how to carry out my duties. Your servant is here among the people you have chosen, a great people, too numerous to count or number. So give your servant a discerning heart to govern your people and to distinguish between right and wrong. For who is able to govern this great people of yours?"

The Lord was pleased that Solomon had asked for this. So God said to him, "Since you have asked for this and not for long life or wealth for yourself, nor have asked for the death of your enemies but for discernment in administering justice, I will do what you have asked. I will give you a wise and discerning heart, so that there will never have been anyone like you, nor will there ever be."

1 KINGS 3:5, 7–12

The disciples came to Jesus and asked, "Who is the greatest in the kingdom of heaven?" Jesus called a little child and had him stand among them. And he said: "I tell you the truth, unless you change and become like little children, you will never enter the kingdom of heaven. Therefore, whoever humbles himself like this child is the greatest in the kingdom of heaven."

MATTHEW 18:1–4

Each one should use whatever gift he has received to serve others, faithfully administering God's grace in its various forms. If anyone speaks, he should do it as one speaking the very words of God. If anyone serves, he should do it with the strength God provides, so that in all things God may be praised through Jesus Christ.

1 PETER 4:10–11

Serve wholeheartedly, as if you were serving the Lord, not men, because you know that the Lord will reward everyone for whatever good he does.

EPHESIANS 6:7–8

Priorities

Jesus said, "If anyone would come after me, he must deny himself and take up his cross daily and follow me. For whoever wants to save his life will lose it, but whoever loses his life for me will save it."

LUKE 9:23–24

Whatever you do, work at it with all your heart, as working for the Lord, not for men, since you know that you will receive an inheritance from the Lord as a reward. It is the Lord Christ you are serving.

COLOSSIANS 3:23–24

Jesus said, "Whoever wants to become great among you must be your servant, and whoever wants to be first must be your slave—just as the Son of Man did not come to be served, but to serve and to give his life as a ransom for many."

MATTHEW 20:26–28

Picture almost 53,000 people screaming, players high-fiving each other, me sweating and grinning and eager to get a drink. It was pandemonium.

I reached down for a cup of water and noticed my son Coy at the back of the table pretending two empty film canisters were cars. He was playing cars, oblivious to the sweat and the blood and the cheers and the uproar. It was almost as if a magnet made me stand there a second longer. I could hardly turn away.

Here I was in the middle of a big game, one that had just turned our way. It was the most important thing in my life. Yet here was truly my life—this little kid who couldn't have cared less whether I won or lost. I was stunned. His priorities had not been screwed up.

It hit me that there were millions of people all over the world who didn't know or care that the Redskins were playing the Chiefs. Really, I wondered, where is the true perspective?

To my son it meant little. And to me, what will mean anything twenty years from now? I may still remember that we won that game, but I may not. One thing I do know, though. I know I'll remember Coy playing cars and showing me what was important.

JOE GIBBS

God's Words of Life on
Provision

How great is your goodness,
  which you have stored up for those
    who fear you,
which you bestow in the sight of men
  on those who take refuge in you, LORD.

PSALM 31:19

Your Father knows what you need before you ask him.

MATTHEW 6:8

The Lord will rescue me from every evil attack and will bring me safely to his heavenly kingdom. To him be glory for ever and ever. Amen.

2 TIMOTHY 4:18

"Even to your old age and gray hairs
  I am he, I am he who will sustain you.
I have made you and I will carry you;
  I will sustain you and I will rescue you,"
  says the LORD.

ISAIAH 46:4

From your bounty, O God, you provided for the poor.

PSALM 68:10

Provision

Every good and perfect gift is from above, coming down from the Father of the heavenly lights, who does not change like shifting shadows.

JAMES 1:17

God has shown kindness by giving you rain from heaven and crops in their seasons; he provides you with plenty of food and fills your hearts with joy.

ACTS 14:17

God's divine power has given us everything we need for life and godliness through our knowledge of him who called us by his own glory and goodness.

2 PETER 1:3

The Lord will keep you from all harm—
  he will watch over your life;
the Lord will watch over your coming and
  going both now and forevermore.

PSALM 121:7–8

No temptation has seized you except what is common to man. And God is faithful; he will not let you be tempted beyond what you can bear. But when you are tempted, he will also provide a way out so that you can stand up under it.

1 CORINTHIANS 10:13

Jesus said, "Look at the birds of the air; they do not sow or reap or store away in barns, and yet your heavenly Father feeds them. Are you not much more valuable than they?"

MATTHEW 6:26

God richly provides us with everything for our enjoyment.

1 TIMOTHY 6:17

If, by the trespass of the one man, death reigned through that one man, how much more will those who receive God's abundant provision of grace and of the gift of righteousness reign in life through the one man, Jesus Christ.

ROMANS 5:17

Our compassionate and gracious Lord has expressed himself by helping his people—by providing a daily supply of food, by remembering his covenant and keeping his promises to make them victorious in conquest, by bequeathing to them the heathen lands around them, by revealing his power. And wonder of wonders, when they continued to grumble and complain against him, he provided a way back to him—a plan of redemption and forgiveness!

My Lord is no less active in my life today. He provides for my basic needs—food, shelter, clothing—by allowing me to serve him through meaningful and fulfilling work. He has blessed me with rich personal relationships with my family and intimate friends. To guide me in facing the hassles of daily living, he has sent his Holy Spirit, and I find myself clinging to him every day.

DON WYRTZEN

Devotional Thought on
Provision

God's Words of Life on
Rest

Let the beloved of the LORD rest secure in
  him, for he shields him all day long, and the
  one the LORD loves rests between
  his shoulders.

DEUTERONOMY 33:12

Find rest, O my soul, in God alone;
  my hope comes from him.

PSALM 62:5

When you lie down, you will not be afraid;
  when you lie down, your sleep will be sweet.

PROVERBS 3:24

I lie down and sleep;
  I wake again, because the LORD sustains me.

PSALM 3:5

The fear of the LORD leads to life:
  Then one rests content, untouched
  by trouble.

PROVERBS 19:23

Rest

Jesus said, "Come to me, all you who are weary and burdened, and I will give you rest. Take my yoke upon you and learn from me, for I am gentle and humble in heart, and you will find rest for your souls. For my yoke is easy and my burden is light."

MATTHEW 11:28–30

He who dwells in the shelter of the Most High will rest in the shadow of the Almighty.

PSALM 91:1

Ask where the good way is, and walk in it, and you will find rest for your souls.

JEREMIAH 6:16

I have set the LORD always before me.
 Because he is at my right hand,
 I will not be shaken.

Therefore my heart is glad
 and my tongue rejoices;
 my body also will rest secure.

PSALM 16:8–9

I will lie down and sleep in peace,
  for you alone, O Lord,
  make me dwell in safety.

PSALM 4:8

In repentance and rest is your salvation,
  in quietness and trust is your strength.

ISAIAH 30:15

My soul finds rest in God alone;
  my salvation comes from him.

PSALM 62:1

By the seventh day [of creation] God had
finished the work he had been doing; so on
the seventh day he rested from all his work.
And God blessed the seventh day and made it
holy, because on it he rested from all the
work of creating that he had done.

GENESIS 2:2–3

God's Words of Life on
Rest

The LORD is gracious and righteous;
  our God is full of compassion.
The LORD protects the simplehearted;
  when I was in great need, he saved me.
Be at rest once more, O my soul,
  for the LORD has been good to you.

PSALM 116:5–7

"My people will live in peaceful dwelling places,
  in secure homes,
  in undisturbed places of rest," says the
LORD.

ISAIAH 32:18

Then, because so many people were coming
and going that they did not even have a
chance to eat, Jesus said to his disciples,
"Come with me by yourselves to a quiet place
and get some rest."

MARK 6:31

God's Words of Life on
Rest

There remains ... a Sabbath-rest for the people of God; for anyone who enters God's rest also rests from his own work, just as God did from his.

HEBREWS 4:9–10

My heart is not proud, O LORD,
  my eyes are not haughty;
I do not concern myself with great matters
  or things too wonderful for me.
But I have stilled and quieted my soul;
  like a weaned child with its mother,
  like a weaned child is my soul within me.

PSALM 131:1–2

On my bed I remember you, O LORD;
  I think of you through the watches of the night.
Because you are my help,
  I sing in the shadow of your wings.

PSALM 63:6–7

Hectic, "rush about" activity takes a heavy stress toll on one's body. You see, God designed my body for camel travel and I keep putting it in subsonic jets! Camel travel allows plenty of time for rest. Subsonic flying keeps me tensed and stressed. Now, I am not saying that we should give up flying in jets! But I am saying we need to recognize that the human frame has its limits, and that we should build in adequate rest and recovery time so as to allow healing and restoration to take place.

This is the problem: People in a hurry never have time for recovery. Their minds have little time to meditate and pray so that problems can be put in perspective. In short, people in our age are showing signs of physiological disintegration because we are living at a pace that is too fast for our bodies. This is the essence of the stress problem.

ARCHIBALD HART

Command those who are rich in this present world not to be arrogant nor to put their hope in wealth, which is so uncertain, but to put their hope in God, who richly provides us with everything for our enjoyment. Command them to do good, to be rich in good deeds, and to be generous and willing to share. In this way they will lay up treasure for themselves as a firm foundation for the coming age, so that they may take hold of the life that is truly life.

1 TIMOTHY 6:17–19

Remember the LORD your God, for it is he who gives you the ability to produce wealth, and so confirms his covenant, which he swore to your forefathers.

DEUTERONOMY 8:18

Wealth and honor come from you, O God;
  you are the ruler of all things.
In your hands are strength and power
  to exalt and give strength to all.

1 CHRONICLES 29:12

God's Words of Life on
Stewardship

[The coming of the Lord] will be like a man going on a journey, who called his servants and entrusted his property to them. To one he gave five talents of money, to another two talents, and to another one talent, each according to his ability. Then he went on his journey. The man who had received the five talents went at once and put his money to work and gained five more. ...

After a long time the master of those servants returned and settled accounts with them. The man who had received the five talents brought the other five. "Master," he said, "you entrusted me with five talents. See, I have gained five more." His master replied, "Well done, good and faithful servant! You have been faithful with a few things; I will put you in charge of many things. Come and share your master's happiness!"

MATTHEW 25:14–16, 19–21

When God gives any man wealth and possessions, and enables him to enjoy them, to accept his lot and be happy in his work—this is a gift from God.

ECCLESIASTES 5:19

Everything comes from you, Lord, and we have given you only what comes from your hand.

1 CHRONICLES 29:14

Give, and it will be given to you. A good measure, pressed down, shaken together and running over, will be poured into your lap. For with the measure you use, it will be measured to you.

LUKE 6:38

"Bring the whole tithe into the storehouse, that there may be food in my house. Test me in this," says the LORD Almighty, "and see if I will not throw open the floodgates of heaven and pour out so much blessing that you will not have room enough for it."

MALACHI 3:10

There is tremendous freedom of mind in knowing and believing that God owns it all, and that money is nothing more than a resource provided by God to allow us to accomplish his purposes on this earth.

Is it wrong then to have a long-term goal of financial independence? I believe not—unless financial independence is defined as having enough to be independent from God. This whole question is really one of "how much is enough?"

How do you achieve one or more of the long-term goals, such as financial independence, college education, improving your lifestyle, getting out of debt, making major contributions or starting your own business? The answer is simple—spend less than you earn and do it for a long time—or as the Bible says, "He who gathers money little by little makes it grow" (Proverbs 13:11).

RON BLUE

Devotional Thought on
Stewardship

Strength

God is our refuge and strength,
 an ever-present help in trouble,
therefore we will not fear, though the earth
  give way
 and the mountains fall into the
 heart of the sea,
though its waters roar and foam
 and the mountains quake with their surging.

PSALM 46:1–3

Do not fear, for I am with you;
 do not be dismayed, for I am your God.
I will strengthen you and help you;
 I will uphold you with my righteous
 right hand.

ISAIAH 41:10

Surely God is my salvation;
 I will trust and not be afraid.
The LORD, the LORD, is my strength
  and my song;
 he has become my salvation.

ISAIAH 12:2

God's Words of Life on
Strength

The foolishness of God is wiser than man's wisdom, and the weakness of God is stronger than man's strength.

1 CORINTHIANS 1:25

The LORD gives strength to his people;
  the LORD blesses his people with peace.

PSALM 29:11

I can do everything through Christ who gives me strength.

PHILIPPIANS 4:13

Do not grieve, for the joy of the LORD is your strength.

NEHEMIAH 8:10

The Sovereign LORD is my strength;
  he makes my feet like the feet of a deer,
  he enables me to go on the heights.

HABAKKUK 3:19

Strength

My flesh and my heart may fail,
  but God is the strength of my heart
  and my portion forever.

PSALM 73:26

The Lord stood at my side and gave me
strength, so that through me the message
might be fully proclaimed.

2 TIMOTHY 4:17

Those who hope in the LORD
  will renew their strength.
They will soar on wings like eagles;
  they will run and not grow weary,
  they will walk and not be faint.

ISAIAH 40:31

I love you, O LORD, my strength.
The LORD is my rock, my fortress and my
  deliverer;
  my God is my rock, in whom I take refuge.
  He is my shield and the horn of my
  salvation, my stronghold.

PSALM 18:1–2

God's Words of Life on
Strength

I pray ... that you may know ... God's incomparably great power for us who believe. That power is like the working of his mighty strength, which he exerted in Christ when he raised him from the dead and seated him at his right hand in the heavenly realms.

EPHESIANS 1:18–20

Jesus said, "My grace is sufficient for you, for my power is made perfect in weakness." Therefore I will boast all the more gladly about my weaknesses, so that Christ's power may rest on me.

2 CORINTHIANS 12:9

Be strong in the Lord and in his mighty power.

EPHESIANS 6:10

A wise man has great power,
  and a man of knowledge increases strength.

PROVERBS 24:5

The Lord gives strength to the weary
  and increases the power of the weak.

ISAIAH 40:29

One thing God has spoken,
  two things have I heard:
that you, O God, are strong,
  and that you, O Lord, are loving.

PSALM 62:11

Nothing is impossible with God.

LUKE 1:37

The Lord is my strength and my shield;
  my heart trusts in him, and I am helped.
My heart leaps for joy
  and I will give thanks to him in song.

PSALM 28:7

I don't like to fail, but I can handle it. That hasn't always been true, but as a Christian of ten years, I know where my strength comes from. I know that even if I give up a home run that makes me a goat, I'll survive. My wife and kids will still love me. God is still in his heaven. The world will not come to an end, regardless of my performance.

It's my faith that lifts me up when I've failed. It's my faith that reminds me of my true insignificance when the world has been laid at my feet because of my success at throwing a ball. To call myself a Christian and then not strive to be the best I can be and do the most I can with what has been given me would be the height of hypocrisy. Being a Christian is no excuse for mediocrity or passive acceptance of defeat. If anything, Christianity demands a higher standard, more devotion to the task.

OREL HERSHISER

Devotional Thought on
Strength

Struggle

Let us fix our eyes on Jesus, the author and perfecter of our faith, who for the joy set before him endured the cross, scorning its shame, and sat down at the right hand of the throne of God. Consider him who endured such opposition from sinful men, so that you will not grow weary and lose heart.

HEBREWS 12:2-3

The LORD will fight for you; you need only to be still.

EXODUS 14:14

Our struggle is not against flesh and blood, but against the rulers, against the authorities, against the powers of the dark world and against the spiritual forces of evil in the heavenly realms. Therefore put on the full armor of God, so that when the day of evil comes, you may be able to stand your ground, and after you have done everything, to stand.

EPHESIANS 6:12-13

The weapons we fight with are not the weapons of the world. On the contrary, they have divine power to demolish strongholds.

2 CORINTHIANS 10:4

God's Words of Life on
Struggle

I have fought the good fight, I have finished the race, I have kept the faith. Now there is in store for me the crown of righteousness, which the Lord, the righteous Judge, will award to me on that day—and not only to me, but also to all who have longed for his appearing.

2 TIMOTHY 4:7–8

Through you we push back our enemies,
   O LORD;
  through your name we trample our foes.

PSALM 44:5

I do not trust in my bow,
  my sword does not bring me victory;
but you give us victory over our enemies,
  you put our adversaries to shame.
In God we make our boast all day long,
  and we will praise your name forever.

PSALM 44:6–8

Endure hardship as discipline; God is treating you as sons. For what son is not disciplined by his father? ... We have all had human fathers who disciplined us and we respected them for it. How much more should we submit to the Father of our spirits and live! Our fathers disciplined us for a little while as they thought best; but God disciplines us for our good, that we may share in his holiness. No discipline seems pleasant at the time, but painful. Later on, however, it produces a harvest of righteousness and peace for those who have been trained by it.

HEBREWS 12:7, 9–11

Consider it pure joy, my brothers, whenever you face trials of many kinds, because you know that the testing of your faith develops perseverance.

JAMES 1:2–3

Dear friends, do not be surprised at the painful trial you are suffering, as though something strange were happening to you. But rejoice that you participate in the sufferings of Christ, so that you may be overjoyed when his glory is revealed.

1 PETER 4:12–13

National Football League coach Joe Gibbs prayed fervently as doctors removed a tumor from inside his wife's skull. She survived the operation and recuperated, yet part of her face remains paralyzed.

"I belong to God," she says. "And I believe he allows things to come into our lives for a reason. Just because I don't know the reason doesn't mean there isn't one. Maybe this has just made me more sensitive to other people with problems."

I'll tell you, going through something like that with the person you love sure makes losing a football game seem trivial. I had asked God why he had let me endure a horrible football season in Tampa. In a small way, I think, he was preparing me for this real trial.

There would be other difficulties in my life but none as difficult or scary as almost losing my wife. I still had a lot to learn about priorities and my faith and my ego, but I could never again say that God hadn't led me through some deep waters to strengthen me for when those new lessons came.

JOE GIBBS

Devotional Thought on
Struggle

Trust in the LORD with all you heart
  and lean not on your own understanding;
in all your ways acknowledge him,
  and he will make your paths straight.

PROVERBS 3:5–6

Trust in the LORD forever,
  for the LORD, the LORD,
is the Rock eternal.

ISAIAH 26:4

When I am afraid,
  I will trust in you.
In God, whose word I praise,
  in God I trust; I will not be afraid.
  What can mortal man do to me?

PSALM 56:3–4

The LORD is good,
  a refuge in times of trouble.
He cares for those who trust in him.

NAHUM 1:7

Those who know your name will trust in you,
for you, LORD, have never forsaken those
who seek you.

PSALM 9:10

May the God of hope fill you with all joy and
peace as you trust in him, so that you may
overflow with hope by the power of the
Holy Spirit.

ROMANS 15:13

Commit your way to the LORD;
  trust in him and he will do this:
He will make your righteousness shine
    like the dawn,
  the justice of your cause like the noonday
  sun.

PSALM 37:5-6

Surely God is my salvation;
  I will trust and not be afraid.
The LORD, the LORD is my strength
    and my song;
  he has become my salvation.

ISAIAH 12:2

God's Words of Life on
Trust

Let the morning bring me word of your
   unfailing love,
 for I have put my trust in you.
Show me the way I should go,
 for to you I lift up my soul.

PSALM 143:8

Let him who walks in the dark,
 who has no light,
trust in the name of the LORD
 and rely on his God.

ISAIAH 50:10

Many are the woes of the wicked,
 but the LORD's unfailing love
 surrounds the man who trusts in him.

PSALM 32:10

It is better to take refuge in the LORD
 than to trust in man.

PSALM 118:8

God's Words of Life on
Trust

Those who trust in the Lord
  are like Mount Zion,
  which cannot be shaken but endures forever.

PSALM 125:1

Fear of man will prove to be a snare,
  but whoever trusts in the Lord is kept safe.

PROVERBS 29:25

You will keep in perfect peace, Lord,
  him whose mind is steadfast,
  because he trusts in you.

ISAIAH 26:3

Blessed is the man who trusts in the Lord,
  whose confidence is in him.

JEREMIAH 17:7

Those who have served well gain an excellent
standing and great assurance in their faith in
Christ Jesus.

1 TIMOTHY 3:13

God's Words of Life on
Trust

Since we have confidence to enter the Most Holy Place by the blood of Jesus, by a new and living way opened for us through the curtain, that is, his body, and since we have a great priest over the house of God, let us draw near to God with a sincere heart in full assurance of faith, having our hearts sprinkled to cleanse us from a guilty conscience and having our bodies washed with pure water. Let us hold unswervingly to the hope we profess, for he who promised is faithful.

HEBREWS 10:19–23

I am still confident of this:
  I will see the goodness of the LORD
  in the land of the living.
Wait for the LORD;
  be strong and take heart
  and wait for the LORD.

PSALM 27:13–14

I trust in you, O LORD;
  I say, "You are my God."
My times are in your hands.

PSALM 31:14–15

Live by the day—aye, by the hour. Put not trust in frames and feelings. Care more for a grain of faith than a ton of excitement. Trust in God alone, and lean not on the reeds of human help.

Serve God with all your might while the candle is burning, and then when it goes out for a season, you will have the less to regret. Continue with double earnestness to serve your Lord when no visible result is before you. Any simpleton can follow the narrow path in the light: faith's rare wisdom enables us to march on in the dark with infallible accuracy, since she places her hand in that of her great Guide.

In nothing let us be turned aside from the path which the divine call has urged us to pursue. Come fair or come foul, the pulpit is our watchtower, and the ministry our warfare; be it ours, when we cannot see the face of God, to trust under the shadow of his wings.

CHARLES SPURGEON

God's Words of Life on
Victory

"Where, O death, is your victory?
Where, O death, is your sting?"
The sting of death is sin,
and the power of sin is the law.
But thanks be to God!
He gives us the victory
through our Lord Jesus Christ.

1 CORINTHIANS 15:55-57

With God we will gain the victory,
   and he will trample down our enemies.

PSALM 60:11-12

   God will swallow up death forever.
The Sovereign LORD will wipe away the tears
   from all faces;
he will remove the disgrace of his people
   from all the earth.
The LORD has spoken.

ISAIAH 25:8

Give us aid against the enemy, O LORD,
   for the help of man is worthless.

PSALM 108:12

When the perishable has been clothed with the imperishable, and the mortal with immortality, then the saying that is written will come true: "Death has been swallowed up in victory."

1 CORINTHIANS 15:54

There will be no more night [in heaven]. [God's people] will not need the light of a lamp or the light of the sun, for the Lord God will give them light. And they will reign for ever and ever.

REVELATION 22:5

Who shall separate us from the love of Christ? Shall trouble or hardship or persecution or famine or nakedness or danger or sword? ... No, in all these things we are more than conquerors through him who loved us.

ROMANS 8:35, 37

We will shout for joy when you are victorious
and will lift up our banners
in the name of our God.

PSALM 20:5

Jesus said, "To him who overcomes, I will give
the right to sit with me on my throne, just as
I overcame and sat down with my Father on
his throne."

REVELATION 3:21

For lack of guidance a nation falls,
but many advisers make victory sure.

PROVERBS 11:14

Everyone born of God overcomes the world.
This is the victory that has overcome the
world, even our faith. Who is it that overcomes the world? Only he who believes that
Jesus is the Son of God.

1 JOHN 5:4–5

In the end, God will always be victorious. Satan may rampage through the world and through the souls of people, with God's inscrutable permission, and cause indescribable disaster and anguish. When he is finished, however, and arrogantly boasts to God, "Look what I've done," God will silence him with his majestic, "And now look what I can do." Then Satan will shamefacedly slink into the corners of his hell while God goes about his work of redemption and restoration.

Oh, yes, we mourn. But we have hope—bright hope for tomorrow, when all who trust in Jesus Christ as Savior will move beyond pain and grief forever because we shall be forever with the Lord.

GERALD OOSTERVEEN

Devotional Thought on
Victory

God's Words of Life on
Wisdom

If any of you lacks wisdom, he should ask God, who gives generously to all without finding fault, and it will be given to him.

JAMES 1:5

The fear of the LORD is the beginning
   of wisdom;
   all who follow his precepts have
   good understanding.
   To him belongs eternal praise.

PSALM 111:10

Praise be to the name of God
   forever and ever;
   wisdom and power are his.
He changes times and seasons;
   he sets up kings and deposes them.
He gives wisdom to the wise
   and knowledge to the discerning.

DANIEL 2:20–21

Know also that wisdom is sweet to your soul;
   if you find it, there is a future hope for you,
   and your hope will not be cut off.

PROVERBS 24:14

God's Words of Life on
Wisdom

The fear of the Lord—that is wisdom,
  and to shun evil is understanding.

JOB 28:28

To the man who pleases him, God gives
wisdom, knowledge and happiness.

ECCLESIASTES 2:26

Get wisdom, get understanding;
  do not forget my words or swerve
    from them.
Do not forsake wisdom, and she will
    protect you;
  love her, and she will watch over you.
Wisdom is supreme, therefore get wisdom.
  Though it cost all you have, get
understanding.

PROVERBS 4:5–7

Those who are wise will shine like the brightness of the heavens, and those who lead
many to righteousness, like the stars for ever
and ever.

DANIEL 12:3

To God belong wisdom and power;
counsel and understanding are his.

JOB 12:13

The fear of the LORD is the beginning
of wisdom,
and knowledge of the Holy One is
understanding.

PROVERBS 9:10

Teach us to number our days aright, O LORD,
that we may gain a heart of wisdom.

PSALM 90:12

I keep asking that the God of our Lord Jesus
Christ, the glorious Father, may give you the
Spirit of wisdom and revelation, so that you
may know him better.

EPHESIANS 1:17

The mouth of the righteous man
utters wisdom,
and his tongue speaks what is just

PSALM 37:30

Wisdom

The quiet words of the wise are more to be
   heeded than the shouts of a ruler of fools.
Wisdom is better than weapons of war.

ECCLESIASTES 9:17–18

The father of a righteous man has great joy;
   he who has a wise son delights in him.

PROVERBS 23:24

The wisdom that comes from heaven is first
of all pure; then peace-loving, considerate,
submissive, full of mercy and good fruit,
impartial and sincere.

JAMES 3:17

He who gets wisdom loves his own soul;
   he who cherishes understanding prospers.

PROVERBS 19:8

Surely you desire truth in the inner parts;
   you teach me wisdom in the inmost place.

PSALM 51:6

If you call out for insight
  and cry aloud for understanding,
and if you look for it as for silver
  and search for it as for hidden treasure,
then you will understand the fear of the LORD
  and find the knowledge of God.

PROVERBS 2:3-5

He who walks with the wise grows wise.

PROVERBS 13:20

Wisdom, like an inheritance, is a good thing
  and benefits those who see the sun.
Wisdom is a shelter
  as money is a shelter,
but the advantage of knowledge is this:
  that wisdom preserves the life of
  its possessor.

ECCLESIASTES 7:11-12

The home is the greenhouse where godly wisdom is cultivated. The power of consistent Christian living in the context of family relationships is the primary spiritual classroom for authentic Christianity. The home is where the majority of behavioral traits—good and bad—are learned, reinforced and passed along to future generations.

A home is filled with fragrant and appealing spiritual riches when each member adopts a servant's spirit. Most family arguments and dissension stem from a failure to yield personal rights. A person filled with the Spirit of Christ strongly desires to serve. He does not seek to establish his own emotional turf but freely edifies and encourages other family members through his servant spirit.

CHARLES STANLEY

Whatever you do, work at it with all your heart, as working for the Lord, not for men, since you know that you will receive an inheritance from the Lord as a reward. It is the Lord Christ you are serving.

COLOSSIANS 3:23–24

The LORD your God has blessed you in all the work of your hands.

DEUTERONOMY 2:7

By hard work we must help the weak, remembering the words the Lord Jesus himself said: "It is more blessed to give than to receive."

ACTS 20:35

Six days you shall labor and do all your work, but the seventh day is a Sabbath to the LORD your God. On it you shall not do any work.

DEUTERONOMY 5:13–14

God's Words of Life on
Work

All hard work brings a profit.

PROVERBS 14:23

Make it your ambition to lead a quiet life, to mind your own business and to work with your hands, just as we told you, so that your daily life may win the respect of outsiders and so that you will not be dependent on anybody.

1 THESSALONIANS 4:11–12

May the favor of the Lord our God rest
   upon us;
 establish the work of our hands for us—
 yes, establish the work of our hands.

PSALM 90:17

Whatever you do, whether in word or deed, do it all in the name of the Lord Jesus, giving thanks to God the Father through him.

COLOSSIANS 3:17

The plans of the diligent lead to profit.

PROVERBS 21:5

The desires of the diligent are fully satisfied.

PROVERBS 13:4

My dear brothers, stand firm. Let nothing move you. Always give yourselves fully to the work of the Lord, because you know that your labor in the Lord is not in vain.

1 CORINTHIANS 15:58

Lazy hands make a man poor,
  but diligent hands bring wealth.

PROVERBS 10:4

From the fruit of his lips a man is filled with good things
  as surely as the work of his hands rewards him.

PROVERBS 12:14

We are God's workmanship, created in Christ Jesus to do good works, which God prepared in advance for us to do.

EPHESIANS 2:10

When God gives any man wealth and possessions, and enables him to enjoy them, to accept his lot and be happy in his work—this is a gift of God. He seldom reflects on the days of his life, because God keeps him occupied with gladness of heart.

ECCLESIASTES 5:19–20

God is not unjust; he will not forget your work and the love you have shown him as you have helped his people and continue to help them. We want each of you to show this same diligence to the very end, in order to make your hope sure. We do not want you to become lazy, but to imitate those who through faith and patience inherit what has been promised.

HEBREWS 6:10–12

Serve wholeheartedly, as if you were serving the Lord, not men, because you know that the Lord will reward everyone for whatever good he does.

EPHESIANS 6:7–8

May the God of peace, who through the blood of the eternal covenant brought back from the dead our Lord Jesus, that great Shepherd of the sheep, equip you with everything good for doing his will, and may he work in us what is pleasing to him, through Jesus Christ, to whom be glory for ever and ever. Amen.

HEBREWS 13:20–21

The man who plants and the man who waters have one purpose, and each will be rewarded according to his own labor. For we are God's fellow workers; you are God's field, God's building.

1 CORINTHIANS 3:8–9

God is a worker. This alone gives us a clue that work itself must be significant, that it must have intrinsic value. For, by definition, God can do nothing that is not inherently good, or else he would violate his own nature and character. The fact that God calls what he does "work" and calls that work "good" means that work has intrinsic worth. Since God himself is a worker, we would expect man, who is created in God's image, to be a worker too.

As a human created in God's image, you are inherently significant and when you work you are doing something that is very Godlike. It is not only God's work that is significant; human work is significant, too. It is something ordained by God. The fact that you work is, in the words of Genesis 1, "very good." Intrinsically good. Valued by God.

DOUG SHERMAN AND WILLIAM HENDRICKS

Devotional Thought on

Work

Jesus said, "Peace I leave with you; my peace I give you. I do not give to you as the world gives. Do not let your hearts be troubled and do not be afraid."

JOHN 14:27

Do not worry about your life, what you will eat or drink; or about your body, what you will wear. Is not life more important than food, and the body more important than clothes? Look at the birds of the air; they do not sow or reap or store away in barns, and yet your heavenly Father feeds them. Are you not much more valuable than they?

MATTHEW 6:25–26

Cast all your anxiety on God because he cares for you.

1 PETER 5:7

The LORD is good,
  a refuge in times of trouble.
He cares for those who trust in him.

NAHUM 1:7

God's Words of Life on
Worry

Jesus said, "Do not let your hearts be troubled. Trust in God, trust also in me."

JOHN 14:1

Trust in the LORD and do good;
  dwell in the land and enjoy safe pasture.
Delight yourself in the LORD
  and he will give you the desires of
  your heart.

PSALM 37:3–4

Do not be anxious about anything, but in everything, by prayer and petition, with thanksgiving, present your requests to God. And the peace of God, which transcends all understanding, will guard your hearts and your minds in Christ Jesus.

PHILIPPIANS 4:6–7

Why are you downcast, O my soul?
  Why so disturbed within me?
Put your hope in God,
  for I will yet praise him,
  my Savior and my God.

PSALM 42:11

God is just: He will pay back trouble to those who trouble you and give relief to you who are troubled, and to us as well. This will happen when the Lord Jesus is revealed from heaven in blazing fire with his powerful angels.

2 THESSALONIANS 1:6–7

Cast your cares on the LORD
  and he will sustain you;
  he will never let the righteous fall.

PSALM 55:22

Commit to the LORD whatever you do,
  and your plans will succeed.

PROVERBS 16:3

Jesus said, "Do not set your heart on what you will eat or drink; do not worry about it. For ... your Father knows that you need them. But seek his kingdom, and these things will be given to you as well."

LUKE 12:29–31

Much of the damaging stress we experience comes from threats that can't be acted on because they exist only in the mind and imagination. Take, for example, the effect of those threats created by worry and anxiety. There are people whose thoughts are so active and bothersome that they constantly imagine the worst. This worrying magnifies actual threats and creates imagined ones. The problem is in the mind, although for the body the threat is real. Further, we don't always recognize our "worry stressors." They hide in the dark hours of the night when we try to sleep or in the unconscious activities of our minds when we are doing our daily chores.

It is these more subtle threats that produce the greatest amount of stress damage. Things that worry us, prod us, scare or frighten us—when there is nothing we can do about them—can be the most destructive of all. Perhaps this is why Jesus told us, "Do not let your hearts be troubled and do not be afraid" (John 14:27).

ARCHIBALD HART

Sources

Arterburn, Stephen and David Stoop, *The Angry Man*. Dallas: Word, Inc.,1991.

Joseph Bayly, *Psalms of my Life*. David C. Cook Publishing Co., 1987.

Buechner, Frederick, *The Magnificent Defeat*. Harper & Row, 1985. Used by permission of HarperCollins Publishers.

Blue, Ron, *Master Your Money*. Nashville: Thomas Nelson Publishers, 1986.

Bonhoeffer, Dietrich, *The Cost of Discipleship*. SCM Press, Ltd. 1959

Boone, Pat, *Pray to Win*. 1980, Used by permission.

Colson, Charles, *Loving God*. Grand Rapids: Zondervan, 1983,1987.

Dravecky, Dave, *When You Can't Come Back*. Grand Rapids: Zondervan, 1992.

Farrar, Steve, *Point Man*. Portland: Multnomah Press, 1990. By permission of Questar Publishers.

Gibbs, Joe, taken from *Joe Gibbs: Fourth and One*. Nashville: Thomas Nelson Publishers, 1991.

Hart, Archibald, *Adrenalin and Stress*. Dallas: Word, Inc., 1991.

Hershiser, Orel, *Out of the Blue*. Wolgemuth and Hyatt, Publishers. Used by permission of NavPress, 1989.

Hicks, H. Beecher, *Correspondence with a Cripple from Tarsus*. Grand Rapids: Zondervan. 1990

Landry, Tom, *Tom Landry: An Autobiography*. Grand Rapids: Zondervan, 1990.

Larson, Bruce. *Dare to Live Now*. Grand Rapids: Zondervan, 1965.

LeSourd, Leonard, *Strong Men, Weak Men*. Chosen Books,1990. Used by permission of Baker Book House.

Lucado, Max, *The Applause of Heaven*. Dallas: The Word, Inc., 1990.

Manning, Brennan, *Lion and Lamb*. Chosen Books,1986. Used by permission of Baker Book House.

Sources

Merton, Thomas, *Life and Holiness*. Abbey of Gethsemani, Inc., 1963.

Oosterveen, Gerald, *Too Early Frost*. Grand Rapids: Zondervan, 1988.

Ben Patterson, *Waiting*. Downer's Grove: InterVarsity Press, 1989.

Peterson, Eugene H., *Run With the Horses*. Downer's Grove: InterVarsity Christian Fellowship of the USA, 1983.

Sherman, Doug and William Hendricks, *Your Work Matters to God*. Used by permission of NavPress, 1987.

Singletary, Mike with Jerry Jenkins, *Singletary on Singletary*. Nashville: Thomas Nelson Publishers, 1991

Smalley, Gary and John Trent, *The Gift of Honor*. Nashville: Thomas Nelson Publishers, 1987.

Smedes, Louis, *Sex for Christians*. Grand Rapids: Wm. B. Eerdmans Publishing Co., 1985.

Spurgeon, Charles, *Lectures To My Students*. Used by permission of HarperCollins Publishers Limited.

Stanley, Charles, *Forgiveness*. Nashville: Thomas Nelson Publishers, 1987.

Stanley, Charles, *A Touch of His Wisdom*. Grand Rapids, Zondervan, 1992.

Swindoll, Charles. *You and Your Child*. Insight for Living, Anaheim, 1986.

Trobisch, Walter, *The Misunderstood Man*. Downer's Grove: InterVarsity Christian Fellowship of the USA, 1983. Used by permission.

Wyrtzen, Don, *A Musician Looks at the Psalms*. Grand Rapids: Zondervan, 1988.

Yancey, Philip, *Disappointment with God*. Grand Rapids: Zondervan, 1988.

A young pastor in Zimbabwe, Africa, later martyred for his faith in Christ. Taken from *The Signature Press of Jesus* by Brennan Manning. Multnomah Press, 1992. Used by permission of Questar Publishers.

Other Titles to enjoy:

God's Words of Life from the NIV Men's Devotional Bible

God's Words of Life for Dads from the New International Version

God's Words of Life for Leaders from the New International Version

Promises for Dads from the New International Version

Dads are a Gift from God

Prayers from a Dad's Heart
  Asking God's Blessings and Protection for your children.

Proverbs for Life for Men